Discover Love

Finding a Marriage That Works

John Lacy

SPIRIT PRESS

Portland, Oregon

Cover design by ICON Communications
Text design by Sheryl Mehary

SPIRIT PRESS
3324 N.E. Peerless Place
Portland, Oregon 97232

This book is dedicated to my wife Kathy with whom I have shared many wonderful years discovering love, to our sons Michael, Scott and David who continue to bless us with love and lessons for life, and to God who taught us what love really is.

Acknowledgements

No book is ever the product of just one mind. There are life experiences brought by others, thoughts expressed by writers and colleagues who share their stories and ideas which shape the material which eventually becomes a book. Some of the people to whom I owe a debt are listed in the Suggested Reading section of this book. Others are anonymous, but have enriched me with reflections, situations and wisdom which I have attempted to pass on to you. Particularly helpful were the comments of my brother, the Rev. James A. Lacy, who is a Presbyterian minister and Pastoral Counselor who helped me with a review of the questions used throughout the book. He bears credit but no responsibility for what I did with his valuable input. I also would like to thank Suzanne Deakins and Spirit Press for editorial suggestions and their belief in this project. And special thanks go to Trisha Lyons and Dan Prow of ICON Communications for their outstanding cover design and encouragement along the way. To all these and especially my family which has supported me in innumerable ways throughout the writing of this book, thank you and may all who read this, Discover Love through all of our efforts.

Table of Contents

Introduction

And now abide these three: faith, hope, and love. But the greatest of these is love.

Saint Paul, I Corinthians 13

How do you discover love…real love…love that lasts? Ever since Adam looked around the garden filled with fascinating plants, lofty trees, and wonderful animals and discovered that he was still lonely, people have been looking for love. We've been looking for that one person—someone who we can love and who will love us back for a lifetime.

Does that ideal exist only in movies or romantic novels? If Daniel Goleman is correct in predicting that sixty-seven percent of all marriages formed in 1990 will end in divorce, then we might be forgiven for thinking that the goal of finding someone to marry for a lifetime is simply unrealistic. On the other hand, you can read every day of some couple who is celebrating their fiftieth wedding anniversary, and they aren't planning on quitting there either. My personal favorite was the ninety-six-year-old "Colonel" and his "bride" who celebrated their seventy-fifth wedding anniversary by repeating their vows and pledging to go for twenty-five more!

So it is possible to find a marriage that works. It is even more likely to happen for you if you take time to know yourself and know everything you can about someone you think might be that love of your life. Failing to ask questions can be the biggest mistake you can make.

Sandy and Peter thought they knew each other well. After all, they had grown up in the same small town and had known each other in school, though he was a couple of years older. They had the same friends, went to the same parties, seemed to have fun together, and they made such a "cute couple." Her parents weren't too thrilled at the idea of her getting married before going to college, but they had never been too successful in denying her anything, and he seemed like a nice boy. His family wasn't against them marrying and agreed that both sets of parents would help if they went on to school. The marriage was on!

A year later, it was over. Sandy had discovered all the things she could have known if she had taken the time to ask. They had almost nothing in common except having a good time at parties. But that was all Peter really wanted to do at college, make the rounds from one party to another. She had ambition and plans for the future; he figured that could wait until the end of senior year. She wanted to go to church; he was too hung over to bother. She had always liked to spend money; he was something of a miser except for spending on his life in the fast lane.

But worst of all she had discovered that his family had covered up a history of violence and infidelity. When he cheated on her, she confronted him. When he started to beat her, she left in the nick of time before he got his hands on the baseball bat. Actually, she was very lucky to get out with her life. She learned to ask questions the next time. In fact, she did remarry someone with whom she had a much better chance of making a successful marriage. But it had been a dangerous detour on the way to discovering real love.

How do you find that someone who is the right one for you—or at least not marry someone really wrong? Everyone says it's a jungle out there. The rate of marriage failure has never been higher. The sad story of spousal abuse pervades the media, revealing an ugly pattern of behavior that is transmitted from one generation to another. Child abuse, drug abuse, and behavior problems resulting from growing up in dysfunctional families render many potential mates really unsuitable for marriage, but how do you know before it's too late and you're sleeping with the enemy?

Often it is the nicest people who seem to fall victim to the attractive but manipulative man or woman. In fact, if you are a kind, trusting, and accepting sort, you may be the perfect victim for the dysfunctional person, who will know how to make you feel protective or sorry for them and hook you into a relationship. At first they may seem to be the most loving, affectionate, and considerate person you ever met. Only afterward will the pain tell you that you made a mistake, but even then you may not be able to figure out what happened. So how can you spot this ahead of time?

Back in the early days of our country when divorce was nearly unknown, marriages were arranged, usually by the family, sometimes with the aid of a matchmaker. The family or the match-maker would ask questions about the relative merits of prospective suitors and would screen out the undesirables from the ones who would make a good husband or wife for their child. The wonderful play *The Matchmaker,* which became the musical *Hello Dolly!,* is about that quaint institution. But amidst all the fun, what is not always clear is that it was an institution that really worked.

It's a different world today. Some marriages are still arranged, and there are a few matchmakers around. The computerized dating services were supposed to take the guesswork out of finding love. But most people are thrown into the business of dating and finding a mate with little help or guidance. Often the advice you hear is misleading or worse. If you take your cues from the soap operas, sitcoms, or talk shows, you will see a world of unreality filled with bizarre relationships that masquerade as normal. Most of the stars that pronounce their opinions on marriage so glibly on Letterman or Sally Jesse Raphael have strange and unhappy lives. The clichés about marriage and romance abound. "They make such a cute couple" is still the recipe for happiness on TV, even though it has been proven over and over that looks have little to do with success in marriage.

This book is born out of hard experience. I spent over twenty-five years counseling couples as they were about to get married, refereeing couples whose marriage was in trouble, and attempting to ease the pain of those going through divorce. In most cases, I could tell you which couples would succeed or fail before they walked down the aisle or out the office door. Throughout the book I have used examples from these sessions, but the names have all been changed and some of the details altered to protect people's privacy. In some cases, the examples represent a compilation rather than a single incident.

In most cases of marital failure, if the couples had asked some very basic questions, they would never have married in the first place. They could have saved themselves the misery, emotional damage, and economic consequences to themselves and their children that divorce (or even the breakup of long-term unmarried relationships) entails. But often they didn't even know the right questions to ask, or they avoided asking them because they were "so in love."

So this book is about questions. They are questions you can and should ask yourself and your intended mate before you get married or move in together. I add "or move in together" because so many couples today seem to be deciding that a "trial marriage" is a good way to find out about a potential mate before you make a mistake. But you might as well know that this idea, which was popularized in the '60s and '70s, has finally been researched enough to see the results of this experiment. So even apart from the moral and religious grounds for preferring real marriage to these live-in arrangements, there is hard data to show that this idea is not working.

In spite of what you may hear, moving in with someone is not a good way of avoiding making a mistake or avoiding the pain of divorce for three reasons:
- *Because the level of commitment is not the same, couples tend to act as if they are still on trial, so you still may not know what your mate is really like. And, of course, the person may not become more committed to marriage later on. Why pay for what you can get for nothing? Why respect someone who gives in so easily? Women tend to be the biggest losers in these relationships in terms of time, money, and parental responsibilities. Very few women ever collect palimony or child support from such non-legal arrangements. This is a big price to pay for a "trial marriage" that may not tell you anything.*
- *Because the emotional involvement is just as intense as in a marriage, live-in arrangements are often just as hard to exit, and the break up is just as emotionally and physically damaging to couples and children as in legal marriages, often more so. The first one I was personally acquainted with ended*

up with an enraged ex-boyfriend coming after his girlfriend, with whom he had lived for only three months, with a handgun. He shot out the windows of one of our local restaurants, nearly killing several customers. He was serious!

- *Thirty years of statistics show live-in relationships have a higher failure rate than marriages, and a higher failure rate if the couple eventually marries. And the rates of domestic violence, child abuse, and murder are higher for these relationships. Don't believe the Hollywood hype!*

So, in this book, you will not hear me talking much about living together. I really don't believe in it. If you want to find real love, you will want to find someone who will be committed enough to you to marry you without any "trial." Love does involve risk. You can eliminate some of the risk by asking the right questions ahead of time. But love involves faith and trust in someone as well, and there is no way to eliminate all uncertainty.

It is tempting to ask, in the face of the dramatically rising divorce rate over the last forty years, just what went wrong? There is no single or simple answer. People blame the automobile, the saturation of our youth culture with sexually charged advertising, music, television programming and movies, affluence, the lack of good role models, and the deterioration of morals in society in general. All of these undoubtedly have had a role to play. But one thing is certain. Society no longer places the stigma it once did on divorce, which for the sake of victims is a good thing, but it also means that society does not protect or value marriage the way it once did. Divorce is considered so normal that many people are now expecting to live through one. A cartoon I saw captured the mood. A young man, in traditional pose on bended knee, proposes to his intended, saying, "Darling, will you be my first wife?"

Of course, if you expect failure, you are paving the way for it. Anyone who goes into a marriage with the mental reservation that "I'll try this, but if it doesn't work out we can always get a divorce," may as well contact a divorce attorney when he or she signs the license. Yet it is understandable, when so many children from divorced families are now getting married, that some of them will have such reservations in the back of their minds. Others may be determined that the mistakes of their parents will not destroy their marriage, but they will not have had the role models of a happy marriage to guide them. There are a lot of factors that are working against having a successful marriage these days. Family background is a very important consideration.

So what does make a marriage work? I could just tick off a list, which would include things like love, good communication, complementary strengths, compatible backgrounds, realistic expectations, and the like, but lots of good books have been written about all of those subjects. The reality is that so often people do not read them until after they are married and are starting to have problems...difficulties that the best book can't necessarily undo, and that they might have avoided had they asked the right questions before they married.

Instead, I'd rather give you the right questions to ask and let you infer some of the qualities that make a good, happy, and successful marriage. I used to say that any two people who were really committed to each other could, with God's help, make a marriage work. That is partly true, but so much of what makes a marriage work is finding the person who loves you enough to work with you, and who has the right blend of qualities and background to fit well with you. Many couples say they are committed to each other, but many either do not have the skills they need or have so many problems that they are not able to make a marriage work. You owe it to yourself to ask some important questions before you marry.

People learn more from asking questions than just hearing answers anyway. Asking these questions will help you, whether you're just starting to date, thinking about getting married for the first time, or starting over again. These questions will also help if you are in a relationship that isn't going well and are wondering why. In addition, I'll give suggestions as to when and where you need to go to get help.

These questions will help you sort out the person who is a

good match for you from those who could spell real trouble. I've tried to keep them simple so that you can work them into conversations. I don't recommend quizzing your intended mate by reading the questions from this book! But do find a way to ask the questions you need to ask him or her directly. Of course, I am assuming that you want to know the answers, and that you will not be satisfied with superficial answers or with someone telling you what they think you want to hear. If you ask the questions in such a way that you let them know the answer you expect, you will defeat the purpose.

I know that it isn't always easy to be rational and realistic about someone you are "in love with." That is why it is important that you take the time right now to go through this book and answer all the questions you can. Be honest. Don't minimize the importance of negative feelings or information you get from the answers. If a person has a bad habit or tendency before they are married, marriage will tend to make it worse, not better. Marriage is not reform school!

And maybe the wedding presents have already started to arrive. It is a lot easier to send them back than to end up fighting over them in a divorce. So if you discover some real red flags going up as you go through these questions, take them seriously. I'll mark the really critical ones that mean you need to get help, take a really deep look, or head for the nearest exit. But you may also find that you have really found the right person, and wouldn't that be reassuring?

Happy hunting! It may be a jungle out there, and there may be pathological liars, cheats, and other predators, but there are also a lot of great people who are worth searching for. I hope this little book will help you find the one who will really love you for a lifetime!

How to Use This Book

Be Prepared

Boy Scout Motto, Sir Robert Baden-Powell

As you will see, I have divided the book into chapters that contain questions you need to answer about yourself and your intended. The questions will be followed by comments that help you to weigh the importance of the answers you get, and some actions you should take as a result. I will also include a set of all the questions in Appendix A so that you can read the questions again, copy them, and reuse them with your intended mate, or go straight through them without going through all the chapters.

I recommend that you go through the book chapter by chapter the first time, answering the questions and reading the comments. I've tried to pack a lot of helpful information into the comments. What you read here is distilled from many years of experience and some of the best research of the last thirty years.

If you are impatient to get into the process, go ahead and use the questionnaire in the back. But before you jump to conclusions, go back and read the comments in the chapters, especially about answers that puzzle you, or questions you may wonder why they were asked. I am really trying to help you uncover the truth about how ready you and your intended mate are to make the step into a permanent relationship.

I do recommend that you either do the questionnaire in pencil or make copies so that you can use this test over and over. You may date a lot of people before you find the prince or princess of your dreams, and this way of evaluating them may become useful many times. I encourage you to evaluate possible mates as early as possible in the dating process, before too much emotional involvement clouds your judgment. A little time spent now can save a wrenching break up later.

If you want to have your mate answer the questions, *do not show him or her the book.* Use the questions from the Appendix A.

You don't want to tip them off to the impact of the answers. It is probably best to ask him or her questions during some of those long talks you ought to be having, and make observations as you get to know their family, friends, and ways of doing things. This shouldn't take any of the fun out of dating. In fact, most people are glad to be asked questions about themselves. Not only will it give them a chance to talk about their favorite subject, but they will also regard you as a brilliant conversationalist!

When should you use this book? Early in the dating process? Later on, when you think you are getting serious? After you get engaged? Well, any time is better than not asking the questions at all, but I feel strongly that the sooner you start evaluating a person as a potential marriage prospect the better. Of course, most people will date someone that they know they won't see after the first date. I once had a blind date with a girl who turned out to be a paratrooper in the army of a nation I won't reveal, and who didn't speak more than a few words of English. I didn't get talked into any more blind dates after that!

She did not make it onto the list of girls I dated in junior high, high school, college, and later that I did think or fantasize about marrying, and that was nearly all of them. Some of them even got a bit serious about me. As I look back, I am so glad I did not marry any of them. God had a much better match in mind. But I was learning to evaluate people as potential marriage partners in that informal process. It helped me recognize the really right person when she finally came into my life.

Relationships have a way of getting serious much faster than we expect. Some people may become much more attracted to you than you are to them and you may find it difficult to get out of the relationship. Or you may find yourself rather quickly getting emotionally involved to the point that you can barely think straight. Or some really romantic but dangerously dysfunctional person can worm their way into your heart and take over your life until you can't get out without a major battle. Preparation can avert disaster.

So even if you aren't dating anyone seriously right now, you can use this book to prepare yourself for the process. If some of these questions stick with you, you can start evaluating anyone you meet as a potential husband or wife. Then when you do find someone in whom you might be interested, you can use the questions from the first or second date on, before you become too emotionally involved to think clearly.

Enough advice. Plunge right in. Here's a way to find that love of your life that even Dolly the matchmaker would approve of!

Chapter 1

How's Your Emotional I. Q.?

Get wisdom; get insight. Do not forsake her, and she will keep you; love her, and she will guard you.

Proverbs 4:6

Nancy stared at nothing in particular as she struggled to regain control. An attractive blonde woman in her thirties, she had three daughters, the oldest a freshman in high school. But as she described her marriage, and her recent discovery that her husband was leaving her for someone else, she finally broke into tears. She tried to make sense of it, tried to place the blame somewhere. They'd married too young, after she'd found out she was pregnant. She had juggled work and babies while he finished school. He'd launched a busy career while she had stayed home raising the family. He had grown, he said, she hadn't. Now it was over, seemingly. I'll never forget the look on her face or the flat, desperate tone in her voice as she said, " You know, the worst of it is I don't even know who I am any more. I don't even know that."

Her story was far too familiar. In the picturesque little Oregon Coast town where I first started out in ministry, I was informed that there was a very high rate of divorce. Not incidentally, there was a high rate of alcoholism, depression, and other family problems. Some blamed it on the long rainy winters and the foggy summers, others on the seasonal nature of the fishing and lumber industries, which left people with a lot of idle time for drinking, becoming depressed, or getting into other kinds of trouble.

But I soon noticed another factor that seemed to be at the heart of the high divorce rate. The prevailing pattern was for young men to graduate from high school, get a job in the local mill, the woods, or on a fishing boat, and then after a couple of years go back to date and marry young women who were just graduating from high school. He was maybe twenty; she was barely eighteen. Neither had much experience of life beyond the confines of their small town. What this produced was a lot of immaturity in marriages.

The men had a bit of practice being on their own and enjoying the freedom and discovering the loneliness of being single, but the women had not. A few years and a couple of kids later, the wife was wondering what had happened to her life. She had lost her freedom, her chance at education or a career, and was mostly at home while he was often as not out with the boys, or at least circulating in the work world. He couldn't understand why she was unhappy (after all, he was bringing home a good paycheck) and why she wanted him to be more than just a provider. She couldn't understand why he couldn't understand. Conflict was inevitable. Many marriages failed.

The point is, usually neither one was emotionally mature enough for marriage. It takes two people who have made a successful job of being single and independent and who have developed emotional maturity to make the give and take of marriage work. Although there are occasional notable successes, teenage marriages have less than a thirty percent chance of lasting.

There are a lot of things that make up what I call our Emotional IQ. Maturity is one of them, and it often has little to do with age. But Daniel Goleman, who coined the term, says it is made up of:

- emotional awareness (the ability to recognize a feeling as it happens),
- mood management (the ability to determine how long a feeling will last and what we will do about it),
- self-motivation (the ability to positively motivate yourself to achieve),
- impulse control (delaying impulses in service toward a goal), and
- people skills (knowing how other people feel and acting appropriately to make friends and get along)

All of these are the marks of a healthy Emotional IQ. Notice that most of the factors Goleman lists are learned skills that are partly related to age, but are also shaped by childhood experiences and family background. Some five year olds will already show many of these skills, while many adults will not. Growing up in a dysfunctional family where mental abuse, physical abuse, or alcohol and drug abuse is present may arrest a child's emotional growth or severely hamper their ability to acquire these skills. Even growing up in families where discipline is lacking or sporadic, or where parents don't model emotional maturity, may hamper a child in learning these traits. Yet these skills are the best predictors of success in academic, professional, and married life.

New studies indicate that high IQ or SAT scores are far less reliable indicators of how well a person will succeed in life than a high Emotional IQ. In other words, it's not how smart you were in school, but how smart you are at handling life that makes the difference. So the questions you will be asking yourself throughout this book will be probing for factors that affect emotional maturity. The answers will tell you if you have the skills and emotional ingredients for making a marriage that works.

So you need to ask some questions:

If you are under 21 ask yourself these questions (if you are over 21 skip these and go to page 6), BE HONEST!:

1. Why do you want to get married right now? List at least three reasons.

   a. _____

   _____

   b. _____

   _____

   c. _____

   _____

2. Have you both completed high school, and are you planning to go on for more education?

   What kind of financial resources do you have that will enable you to get that education? (Will parents help?)

3. What kind of financial resources do you have now that will enable you to live the way you would like to live?

Comments

Question 1: If anywhere among the reasons you give for getting married is "to get out of a bad situation at home," you may well be ready to leave home, but you are not ready to get married. This goes for your prospective mate too. If either one of you have an abusive, alcoholic or violent home life, you have alternatives—good ones—to getting married or moving in with someone.

Go to a guidance counselor, minister, rabbi, or priest and tell them in confidence about your problem. You may be able to live with a friend's family, get your family into counseling, or make some other arrangement for getting out of a bad situation or dealing constructively with it. But if you go into a marriage to escape, you will simply transfer all of the emotional wreckage you carry with you to the new relationship, and you will somehow expect that your mate will be able to heal all of that. Often you will tend to repeat in your own marriage the patterns that you hated in the bad situation. You need help, not escape. Please get it!

If one of the reasons you listed was that you or your mate is pregnant, this is also one of the worst reasons for getting married, especially if you are under eighteen or even twenty-one. You have alternatives, especially if one of you isn't really thrilled about getting married or being a parent. Be very realistic about this. Do both of you really want to get married and be parents? The father is responsible for supporting the baby even if you do not get married. The mother can get court orders defining that support. Her chances of collecting it may not be good, but enforcement is improving. One or both of you will have to interrupt your education in order to raise your child during its early years. Do you want to do that? Are your parents really willing to help out so that one or both of you can finish school?

You will also be told that you have the alternatives of adoption or abortion. Abortion may seem like the quickest, easiest, and most final solution, but many women experience long-term emotional consequences as a result. Adoption can be heart wrenching, but if handled well, it can also give children a wonderful future with someone who really can love and cherish them. You can make a childless couple wonderfully happy. You have more say now than you used to in dealing with the prospective new parents, and ensuring that somewhere down the line your child knows that you loved him or her but were not able to raise them. Religious organizations or groups offering abortion alternatives can give you help in making your decision. You can find them in the phone book under Abortion Alternatives or Adoption.

But unless you and your mate are really sure you want to be married and are ready to make all the sacrifices necessary to raise children, and unless you have plenty of family and financial support, you should seriously consider other alternatives. If you are considering not getting married but keeping the child, understand that seventy-five percent of single unwed teenage mothers do not end up completing their high school education. They often end up in very low paying jobs and live in poverty or on welfare. The alternatives may be difficult, but the consequences can be a lot better for you and the child.

Question 2 and 3: How do you really want to live? It will be on a poverty level without education or skilled training. Don't romanticize here. If either one of you have not completed high school, you have not completed the absolute minimum amount of education you will need to get even an entry-level job. If you want a better job you will need more education. How do you intend to get that?

Unless parents or other family will help, you may find it very difficult to go to school and work at the same time. It will probably be impossible if you are also trying to raise a baby. If you want a comfortable house, a family, and a lifestyle equal to or better than what you've known growing up, how will you earn enough money to get that? And what do you want for your children? The latest U.S. Government statistics estimate that it will cost 1.27 million dollars to raise a child and send him or her through college! Waiting may be difficult, but it will really pay off in the long run. It can give you that maturity and experience of independent living that you will need to face the challenges of life together.

If you are over 21, answer these questions:

1. Have you had at least one year of living on your own (paying your own bills, managing your own life and work) outside a school or college setting? _____
   Has your prospective mate? _____
   How well did each of you manage? _____
   _____

2. Who (or what) does he or she put first in their life? Second? Third? Who (or what) do you put first?
   (Answer this as you see him/her and yourself; then ask him/her to answer.)

Your Answer about Mate	Your Mate's Answer	Your Own Values
God	God	God
Parents	Parents	Parents
Friends	Friends	Friends
You	You	Your mate
Self	Self	Self
Work	Work	Work
Play (hobbies, sports, etc.)	Play (hobbies, sports, etc.)	Play (hobbies, sports, etc.)
Money	Money	Money
Success	Success	Success

Are the differences significant? _____
(See comments.)

3. How does he/she solve problems? (If answers vary depending on the person or situation involved, note who or what seems to make the difference.)
   __ Directly, meets problems head on and solves them
   __ Indirectly, gets around a problem rather than solving it directly
   __ Avoidance, ignores problem and hopes it will go away
   __ Manipulation, cons or scams their way out of a situation
   __ Blusters, shouts or bullies their way out of problem
   __ Drinks or takes drugs to forget the problem, or to make themselves feel better
   __ Blames other people or circumstances for the problem

Do you like the way they solve problems?
Yes   No   Don't know

Does it fit well with the way you solve them?
Yes   No   Don't know

4.   Is he or she ever verbally abusive, especially toward you? (Do you feel put down or in the wrong around them? Does he or she say you're stupid, worthless, etc.? Do they always have to be right, even at your expense?)
    __ Sometimes
    __ Never
    __ Always (or a lot)
    __ Enough to make me uncomfortable

5.   How would you describe his or her personality? *(Check all that apply)*
    __ Ambitious
    __ Easy going, laid back
    __ Control freak, always has to be in control of situations and you
    __ Happy-go-lucky, never worries about anything
    __ Intense, serious about everything
    __ Comfortable to be around
    __ Quiet, never talks much about themselves or feelings
    __ Moody, lots of ups and downs
    __ Predictable, steady
    __ Sociable, gets along well with other people
    __ Unpredictable, never know what they will be doing next
    __ Jealous, gets very angry if he/she thinks you are flirting (when you're not)
    __ Helpful, kind to others
    __ Self-centered, puts his or her needs first
    __ A rescuer, often leaps in to save a situation and gets in over their head to the point where you have to bail them out
    __ Forgetful, absent-minded
    __ Mature, dependable, responsible
    __ Good sense of humor, can laugh at themselves
    __ Immature, pouts or throws tantrums when they don't get their way
    __ Irresponsible, changes jobs a lot, careless about things and promises

__ Cutting sense of humor, uses put downs or racial slurs, tells dirty jokes

__ Uncomfortable, sometimes you feel like you are walking on eggshells

__ Angry, violent, picks fights, pushes you around and blames it on you

Go back and circle any personality traits that you **don't** like or make you uncomfortable.

Will he or she be fun to live with? Yes No Not sure

6. How does he or she handle conflict or frustration?

__ Directly, deals with the person or situation and works for a resolution

__ Indirectly, may not confront a person directly, but works out a solution

__ Avoidance, never deals with the person or situation and hopes it will go away

__ Manipulation, uses you or others to get their way

__ Irresponsible, blames someone else for problem

__ Passive/aggressive, is sneaky, plots revenge

__ Gets angry, fights or bullies their way out

__ Drinks or takes drugs to forget the problem or to make themselves feel better

7. How does he or she get along with other people? *(Check all that apply)*

__ A loner, doesn't like to be around others

__ Not a loner, but doesn't like crowds, gets along well in small groups

__ Is comfortable mostly with family (Theirs? Yours?)

__ Doesn't really get along with other people on the job

__ Gets along well with others in most settings

__ Gets along with other people on the job

__ Is the life of the party, likes to be in the center of things

__ Gets along well with others, people like and trust him or her

8. What is their basic mental attitude? *(Check all that apply)*
    __ Positive, hopeful
    __ Cheerful, optimistic
    __ Moody, ups and downs
    __ Healthy, feel like they are well most of the time
    __ Stressed, tired, overwhelmed by life
    __ Anxious, worried about everyone's feelings, the future,
    etc.
    __ Driven, angry
    __ Gloomy, depressed, sick a lot
    __ Negative, pessimistic

9. Is he or she basically truthful?   Yes   No
    Has he or she ever told you something you found out later
    wasn't true?   Yes   No
    Was it important?   Yes   No
    Does he or she exaggerate about achievements or abilities?
    Yes   No
    Does he or she exaggerate about how pretty or sexy they
    are?   Yes   No
    Is he or she secretive about money, background, family?
    Yes   No
    Does he or she often have to explain away things?
    Yes   No
    Has he or she ever cheated on you?   Yes   No

10. Is life around him or her frequently chaotic? (Are they
    always changing plans at the last minute, trying to do too
    many things at a time, overdoing things, trying to please
    even people who don't matter, or involving you in rescuing
    them from situations they have created?)   Yes   No

Comments:

Question 1. If the answer to this is yes for both of you, this is a good sign you are ready to put a marriage together. You are much better prepared for life together if you have coped well with life as a single person. You will have the self-confidence and knowledge to handle a lot of the challenges you will need to face. If one or the other of you has not been on their own for a while, you might want to wait and not rush into marriage immediately. Otherwise one of you may really feel you missed out on something when the responsibilities of home and family get heavy.

Many couples get married immediately after finishing college, not realizing that college can be a pretty sheltered existence. If one or both of you lived in a dorm, fraternity, or sorority where all meals were provided, and if your parents or scholarships took care of all the bills, you haven't really been on your own in the sense that you will be as a married couple. Take a year to find out if you can handle those responsibilities. You'll be glad you did.

If one of you was on their own but really didn't handle it well, you need to ask why. Is he or she attempting to escape their responsibilities by marrying you? Are there bad habits, bad company, or bad problems you won't want to deal with at the root of that experience? Don't assume that living with you is going to cure any major problems. If he's a slob now, do you want to be picking up after him twenty years from now? If she couldn't manage her finances while single, will she be able to do better when she marries you? You cannot expect a person to change a basic attitude or lifestyle just because they get married. In fact, you should assume that whatever problem they have will get worse.

Question 2. These ratings call for some discernment. How well does your intended see himself or herself? Do they see themselves as you see them? Is there a large discrepancy in the way they think they are and the way they really act? People do tend to see themselves as better than they are (unless they are depressed or mentally ill), but if they have a really unrealistic view of themselves, that is a danger signal. It means that they are not aware of reality and probably not accurately aware of the perceptions of others. Both are important components of Emotional I.Q.

Who or what ranks highest? Where do you rank on the list? If the answers tell you that you are low on your mate's priority list, that tells you something extremely important. Emotionally mature people can put another person first in a healthy way without resentment. In fact, that is really one of the definitions of love. So if he or she tells you that you are first on their list but their actions don't match up, they are showing that they do not really love you, and you cannot expect that to change. If work, golf, or anything else except God comes ahead of you, how long do you think you will enjoy being married to that person? How do you think they will be as a parent?

Question 3. This section may seem self-explanatory, but only the first two choices in the first part of the question involve healthy styles of problem solving. The others involve manipulation or some way of escaping reality. Pay close attention to the second half of the question. Are you comfortable with the way he or she solves problems? If his or her style involves manipulation, avoidance, blaming other people, or drinking and drugs, you are in for big trouble down the line. Life is just full of problems you will need to solve together. And if their style involves not solving problems or creates more problems, guess who will be doing all the solving? Why marry someone who will cause you more problems rather than help you solve crises together?

Question 4. This is a red flag question. The answer needs to be *never.* If he or she is verbally abusive now, when they should be on their best behavior, it will only get worse after you are married (or move in together). You deserve better. No one who says they love you should tell you that you are stupid, worthless, a slut, a slimeball, or make you feel like any of those things. Verbal abuse often leads to physical abuse. Seventy percent of victims of physical abuse become so addicted to the pattern that they cannot get free of the abuser. Too often, someone ends up dead! If you take verbal abuse now it means that you somehow feel like you deserve it, and that means you need to get help right now! Break off the relationship and get help from a counselor, minister, rabbi, or priest, or call an abuse helpline **right now.** Your life may depend on it.

Question 5. There are many personality traits that are not on this list. They will probably show up elsewhere. There ought to be far more positive than negative ones here if you have found the right person for you. You might want to rate yourself on this scale or have your prospective mate rate you. After all, it takes two to make a happy marriage. You shouldn't necessarily have personalities that are alike; in fact it might be boring if you did. But you should have complementary strengths and traits. If one of you is very ambitious and the other is not, your marriage will work provided one of you isn't trying to remake the other. Or if one is sociable but the other is not, your marriage can work, but only if each of you allows the other to be themselves and not push them into being like you.

But there are some traits that are real danger signals here. It is very hard to live with a controller, a liar, a rigid perfectionist, or someone who is very moody, uncomfortable, or irresponsible. It is downright **dangerous** to live with someone who could be described as a loner, a control freak, insanely jealous, violent, immature, and who also drinks or takes drugs. Look these traits over carefully. Don't minimize the importance of negative information. If you don't like these traits now, what makes you think they will change? Will you like them better when you have to live with them in close quarters day in and day out?

Our personalities are mostly formed by the ages of six to eight. We change slowly after that, if at all, so don't assume your intended will change. Look at his or her parents. In what way is he or she like them? Do you like the one he or she is like? If there are some danger signals here, get help, or run—don't walk, to the nearest exit. You haven't found the right one yet.

Question 6. This question may sound a lot like Question 3. But conflict is a step above problem solving. Life is full of challenges, but we often have the most trouble dealing with conflict with another person. The first two ways are the best solutions as they lead to some kind of a solution. The last six generally lead to more problems. Avoidance, manipulation, irresponsibility, and passive/aggressive behavior make the kind of communication that is necessary to solve problems and reduce conflict impossible. Violence and drug or alcohol abuse are destructive and self-destructive ways of dealing with conflict. If they are the way your prospective mate deals with conflict, they need help that you are not qualified to give. If they deal with others that way, be sure that they will end up treating you the same way. **Do not marry or move in with someone who deals with conflict in these ways until after they have gotten long-term help.** Better yet, find someone else. You deserve better!

Question 7. How your prospective mate gets along with other people will say a lot about how he or she will get along with you, and a family. It also will tell you how he or she will get along financially, get ahead in a career, and will match up with you. It is an important component of Emotional I.Q. If you are gregarious and like to be with lots of people while he or she doesn't, how much of that sociability are you willing to give up? If you can find ways to make both of you happy doing your own things separately, fine. But if you want your mate with you when you socialize, this one won't be the right one for you.

Beware the loner or the very antisocial person, unless that is your style too. But often that style may mask some very deep problems. All too often, "real loner" is the description of the serial killer, the assassin, the stalker, the bomber, the sex addict, or the child abuser. If his or her only friends are members of a paramilitary organization, an extremist cult, or an Internet chat room, this could be the warning you need to get out now!

Question 8. How is he or she most of the time? Everyone has down days or bad days. But if you find yourself describing your intended as moody, down, or stressed a lot, you are in for a rough ride down the road. Moodiness may be a sign of chronic depression, the result of being a child of alcoholic or abusive parents, codependency, or bipolar disorder (see Glossary). All of these conditions require therapy and long-term help. Don't dismiss moodiness as something that will go away after marriage. There could be something seriously wrong that you need to investigate. See the comments about Question 10.

Particularly dangerous are people who could be described as angry, or hot tempered a lot of the time. These are early but clear telltale signs of a violent personality, and that violence will be directed at you eventually. Happiness is a choice. People who are basically upbeat about life tend to stay well, achieve more, and have happier marriages and families. I'd rather live with a happy, optimistic person than a grump, wouldn't you?

Question 9. This is a bottom-line question. Communication is the name of the game in marriage. Honesty is what makes communication real. But even more important, being honest to you says that your mate respects himself or herself and respects you. And it isn't just in the big things that honesty is important. I knew a young woman who told her intended that she had obtained a chair in Africa on a trip she had made during college. It turned out that she had never been there and was just trying to impress him. Later, it became clear that she lied about many other things, exaggerated her abilities to get ahead at work, and twisted stories so that she always came out ahead. Her untruthfulness was a great part of the unraveling of that marriage.

The moral? If your intended lies to you even once, it is time to call a halt. The same goes for cheating. Get counseling, make it clear that you won't tolerate lying or cheating, or get out. But **don't let this danger signal go past without doing something about it!**

Question 10. If the answer to any of these examples is yes, you may be dealing with a classic codependent. If their family history has alcoholism, abuse, trauma, or mental illness in the background, adult children of such families are very often codependents whose lives are chaotic. They are rescuers who create situations in which they can rescue or be rescued.

Their spouses usually have no clue about what is driving them, but they often get sucked into the whirlwind of this person's unpredictable lifestyle. Everything, no matter how simple, becomes a "big deal." Any family occasion turns into an overly complicated event. People he or she has every reason to hate are overly entertained or flattered. Gifts are over-elaborate and expensive. The person actually seems to thrive on conflict and chaos. They usually are a combination of the control freak who has to manage everything and the person who is out of control.

Alcoholics Anonymous' definition of a codependent is someone who, when drowning in a river, sees someone else's life flash before their eyes! There really isn't a compact definition of codependency because there are so many symptoms. Some codependents are alcohol and drug abusers themselves; some don't drink but act like alcoholics in terms of their lack of self-control and wild mood swings. They will be in denial and make excuses for the most outrageous behavior by their alcoholic or abusive parents or relatives. But one sure symptom is that life is chaotic around them.

If you find yourself always rescuing your intended from some situation they have created, or making a lot of excuses for their behavior, you are probably dealing with codependency (and you are getting sucked into the codependency game yourself). These people need help beyond what you can give them. They need therapy and groups similar to AA. Unless they get long-term help, you won't want to live with them. There is, unfortunately, a lot of this disease going around, and it is very difficult to cure. **If they won't get help, run—don't walk, to the nearest exit!**

So how is your Emotional IQ? How is your intended's? Will they be fun to live with, or is there a lot of pain ahead? Maturity and personality traits hold the key to the answers, but there are more questions to ask. Press on! The right love for you is out there.

Chapter 2

Alcohol and Drugs

Better to sleep with a sober cannibal than a drunken Christian.

Herman Melville, Moby Dick

Rob looked at me. We had nearly come to the end of the session and hadn't accomplished much. He was a very smart person, a former State Department consular employee and lawyer with a beautiful and talented wife. He taught Sunday school and was faithful in attending church. To all outward appearances he was successful, but his marriage was very definitely going under. His wife had attended only one counseling session and hadn't been very communicative. She was from a Latin American country and seemed to want to return. They had met when he was stationed in her country and had seemed to have much in common, but now she seemed determined to leave him.

Since she refused to come for more counseling, there was little I could do but try to help Rob through the pain. They had separated at this point, and he was really coming apart. Suddenly, he shifted the subject and admitted to having become involved with a girl at his work who was now accusing him of making unwanted advances at an office party. He was afraid he was going to lose his job. He admitted to having too much to drink. Rather belatedly, alarm bells started going off. I hadn't known he drank, especially since he was pretty emphatic about keeping all the commandments to his Sunday school students. He managed to make it sound like this was an isolated event. But as he left, I had the uneasy feeling that I had missed something important.

I moved across the country, he got a job back in the Foreign Service, and we lost touch, except for a Christmas card that told me he had remarried. Three years later and a continent away from where we had started, I got a phone call from an alcohol rehabilitation center. It was Rob. The head of his department had sent him there because his second marriage was falling apart and he was out of control on the job. He wanted to see me when he got a pass, and tell me what he was finding out about himself.

We met and we talked (or rather, he did) nonstop. He was elated at his newly found sobriety, and full of insights that would have seemed so obvious to anyone else but were the product of finally seeing life without the distorted lens provided by the bottom of a bottle. We talked about his marriage and the small boy who was his son. He was hopeful that perhaps he could put his life back together with his family. We parted on that note.

Over the years, I heard from Rob that he had gone through therapy to cure the problems that the alcohol had masked, and he had managed to salvage his marriage and become a real father to his son. I remarked to him how badly I felt that I had missed the signs of addiction when we had first known each other. But he said, "Hey, I was so good at hiding it that I didn't know I had a problem myself, and I wasn't going to let you know either!"

Rob's story seems to have had a happy ending, but with an alcoholic, you never know. Alcohol and drugs have destroyed many a marriage. Something that starts out as just something people do at parties or when they go out together ends up making life an absolute hell later on. No one who starts out taking a drink or getting high ever thinks they are going to get hooked. But some people find their lives becoming more and more centered around drinking or getting drugs, and everything else, including the people they say they love, comes in a distant second.

A person does not have to be a stumbling drunk to be an alcoholic. In fact some people fool themselves and many others by being able to handle an enormous amount of alcohol without showing many obvious symptoms. But addicts are addicts. In their lives, their drug of choice comes first. It colors all of their decisions. It confuses, twists, and destroys all other relationships. If you marry a person with an addiction, you are in for the worst roller coaster ride of your life.

Some people can drink and not become addicted. Some people have a predisposition to alcoholism and should never start. Some people have personalities that seem to make them prone to addiction. People who are related to alcoholics have a four to seven times greater chance of becoming an alcoholic than those who aren't. But how do you find out?

The addict is the last person to know that they have a problem. They are in deep denial by the time you may spot the problem. They will tell you that they can quit anytime and they actually believe they can. But they don't and they won't. You have to observe their behavior and decide whether what they say about their drinking or drug use is true.

If you have a problem yourself, or are participating in their lifestyle, you won't be able to see whether they have stepped over the line into addiction. So here are some self-test questions that have been used by alcohol treatment programs over the years to help a person determine whether they have a drinking or substance abuse problem.

The National Council on Alcoholism and Drug Abuse lists these seven questions: *(Answer them for yourself, then answer how you think your intended mate would answer them.)*
1. Are you having more financial, work, school, or family problems as a result of your drinking (or drug use)?

2. Can you handle more alcohol (or drugs) now than when you first started?

3. Have any of your blood relatives ever had a problem with alcohol (or drugs)?

4. Have you ever been unable to remember part of a previous evening, though your friends say you didn't pass out?

5. Do you drink heavily (or use drugs) when you are disappointed or are under pressure or have had a quarrel with someone?

6. Have you sometimes failed to keep promises you made to yourself about controlling or cutting down? Have you had any legal problems related to your drinking (or taking drugs)?

7. Do you sometimes have the shakes in the morning and find that it helps to have a little drink, tranquilizer, or medication of some kind?

To which I'll add another standard one: Do you find yourself thinking about the next time that you will be able to have a drink or a hit? Do you plan activities around when and where you will be able to get a drink or hit?

If the answer to *any* of these is yes, it indicates a serious drinking or drug problem. This is a test to which only the person with the problem will have the answers, but often they are in denial and won't or can't answer them honestly. If you answered no for yourself to all of the questions, you can make accurate observations about your potential mate. How would you say they should answer those questions?

These observations are important because it matters far more what they **do** than what they **say.** There are a million great lines drinkers use to kid themselves and others about their problem. One woman put it: "I had my drinking under control. I only drank on days beginning with the letter T: Tuesday, Thursday, today, and tomorrow!" Society often laughs with them rather than confronting the problem. But laughing doesn't help, and you need to know if there is a problem before you marry into the world of the alcoholic or addict.

Here are some more questions to help you assess whether your potential mate has a problem you should be concerned about. *(Circle or check answers that apply.)*

1. Does he or she drink? Take drugs? Both? Both at once?
    (If no to all, skip to Question 4 and 5)
    If yes, how much? 1–2 drinks a day   3–4   5 or more
    Until he/she gets drunk/stoned   Until he/she passes out

2. How often does he or she drink and or take drugs?
    __ Only on weekends or social occasions
    __ Has a drink or two daily (wine with a meal)
    __ Often has more than two daily
    __ Parties a lot, tends to get drunk when he or she does
    __ Seems to always need to have a drink or something to feel high
    __ Drinks at home even when no one is around
    __ Goes on binges, a day or more at a time

3. Why would he or she say they drink/take drugs?
    __ To be social, fit in with the crowd
    __ Makes them feel more relaxed, more able to shine socially
    __ Helps them to forget troubles
    __ Helps them to have a good time
    __ Makes life feel better when pressures get to them

4. Is there alcoholism in his or her immediate family?
    Yes   No
    If so, do they talk about it?   Yes   No
    Has the drinker gotten help?   Yes   No
    Did your mate ever go to Alateen or Al-anon?   Yes   No
    Did they get other help?   Yes   No

5.   Is your prospective mate a recovering alcoholic/drug addict? Yes No
     If yes, how long have they been sober ____?
     Are they in some kind of support or therapy? _____
     Did they quit therapy? _____
     Why?_____

6.   How do they treat other people when they are drinking/taking drugs?
     __ Mellow out, withdraw, fall asleep
     __ Get boisterous, rowdy, embarrass you
     __ Get sullen or mean
     __ Get violent, paranoid, start fights

7.   When he or she enjoys hobbies or activities, is it partly or mostly because they offer an excuse to drink or take drugs? (Is the tailgate party more important than the game?)
     Yes No Maybe

8.   What excuses do they give for behaving badly, missing work, forgetting appointments, etc.? _____
     _____
     Does drinking or drug taking have something to do with it?
     Yes No

Comments:

The self-test by the National Council: If in going through the questions you discovered that you might have a problem, your first priority needs to be to get help. You are not ready to get married or handle a relationship with anyone unless you get help right now. And there are no quick fixes. Until a person has passed a year of sobriety, Alcoholics Anonymous (AA) recommends that they not enter into a marriage or heavy relationship. You are doing yourself, your potential mate, and children a huge favor if you explain to them that you have found out that you need to get help for your alcohol problems and that any future relationship with them will have to be put on hold until you are clean and sober for at least six months after rehab. If he or she is the right person for you, they will wait for you to go through treatment. They will be supportive and will be willing to go to Al-anon (the support group for spouses and adult children of alcoholics) meetings so they can understand how and how not to support you.

If you suspect that your potential mate has a drinking problem from what you think his or her answers should be on the self-test, and you get indications from the next set of questions that confirm this, you face some pretty tough choices based on some very tough information. The first thing to realize is that *you* cannot cure an alcoholic or drug addict, no matter how much you love them. You may be able to confront them with the need to get help. You may be able to be supportive of them if they decide to get help (for example by going to Al-anon meetings that help you understand their problem). But you can't make them stop drinking or seek a cure. They have to do that themselves.

Often, the most constructive thing you can do is to remove yourself from the situation. You can tell them you love them, but that they have a problem for which they need to get help, and that you are not going to contribute to it by pretending that it isn't a problem. Give them the number of Alcoholics Anonymous or some other substance abuse hotline number, and tell them you are not going to be involved with them until they have obtained serious help.

You will have to mean it, and you will have to steel yourself against all sorts of emotional appeals, excuses, and attempts to win you back by half-hearted measures, like going to one or two meetings and pronouncing themselves cured. These are the stock-in-trade of every person with an addiction problem. They will not be into recovery unless they admit they have a problem, get into therapy and/or a program, and spend more than six months afterward clean and sober or drug free. *At this point, there should be noticeable changes in behavior.* If not, the person is not taking rehab or you seriously.

If you decide not to put yourself through that long-term process, that is certainly justifiable. You are not responsible for their problem. There are really no guarantees that any person with a drinking or drug problem will seek the treatment they need, stay with it long enough to be "cured," and be the kind of person you'll want to live with when they do. Once the drinking or drugs are eliminated, the person may be harder to live with than before because repressed behaviors surface and other problems emerge. If going to meetings for the rest of your life, or spending your days wondering if your mate is going to slip off the wagon is not your idea of the way you want to spend your life, now is a good time to get out of the relationship. You should tell them why, and suggest getting help, but you are not responsible for rescuing them.

Perhaps you may think I am overly pessimistic at this point. Don't take my word for it. Go to your nearest Al-anon meeting and talk to the wives of an alcoholic or drug addict. There is nothing like the voice of experience. Alcoholics and drug addicts can and do recover, but living with them while they are going through it is a real struggle. If you aren't already married to an addict, why would you want to put yourself through that? There are better possibilities around.

Comments on the second set of questions: These are designed to give you a better handle on the existence and severity of your potential mate's problem. If you are not sure of the answers, it is a good idea to do some double-checking. For instance, if you don't know whether there is a drinking problem in your mate's family, and they won't say or they minimize it, ask some other people who know them what they think.

Question 1. If the answer to all of these is No, consider yourself fortunate, and skip down to 4 and 5. If it is Yes, then the most serious problems result when people mix drugs and drink. How much and how often becomes critical in assessing the depth of the problem, but mixing drugs can be fatal. Many a celebrity has died recently of imbibing a "cocktail" mixture of drugs and alcohol, not knowing what lethal reactions could occur. It only takes once.

This is the equivalent of playing Russian roulette, and sometimes indicates suicidal desires. This person needs help desperately.

The "How much?" questions can give you a yardstick by which to measure a person's tolerance and behavior. Even though there has been recent evidence that very moderate drinking can lower the risk of heart disease, the AMA still recommends only a maximum of two drinks per day for a male, one for a female. Most authorities tend to regard one to four drinks at a social function as social, not problem, drinking.

Legally, you may have exceeded the blood alcohol limit at two drinks, depending on your height and weight and the amount of time elapsed. Beyond that, a high tolerance is being indicated when someone drinks more than four drinks, *especially if they don't show much effect.* Binge drinking, where a person drinks steadily for more than a day, or disappears on a drunk for days, is the most severe indicator of a problem, but when a person drinks primarily to get drunk, they are on their way to severe problems.

Question 2. When and how often the person drinks is crucial. Only the first two answers are indicators of non-problem drinking, though the third may not indicate a major problem yet. Any of the other answers are indicators of severe drinking problems. Obviously, you may not know if a person drinks alone at home, unless you find a lot of empties when there hasn't been a party or smell alcohol on the breath at early hours of the day. But any attempt to hide their drinking from you or others is a good indicator that they drink more than they want to admit. I knew a very prim Sunday school teacher who kept her Vodka in a peanut butter jar in the refrigerator so people wouldn't know what she was up to! Women are more prone to drink alone at home than men, but having a stash is a good indicator that drink or drugs have taken over.

Question 3. Why a person drinks is most important, and the differences in these responses are subtle but important. If a person drinks to be social or to fit in with the crowd, he or she is responding to peer pressure. Particularly when people are younger this is a powerful motivation, but there is the hope that they will grow out of this and that the values of marriage and family will become more important. However, you will need to discuss what part drinking will play in your marriage and pay close attention to what they say and do.

If they say that drinking makes them feel more socially adept, brighter, or more "with it," that is quite a different thing. They are saying that they need alcohol to do for them something they don't feel they can do for themselves. Alcohol or drugs become a necessity to make them feel good about themselves. This is addictive reasoning. They need to get help with why they feel the way they do about themselves or they will slip over the line into alcoholism or drug addiction.

The same is true of the rest of the reasons. When someone depends on alcohol or drugs to fill some psychological need, you are dealing with addiction. One other question you might do well to ask is *when* the person started to drink. In general, the earlier they started, the more rapidly a person will develop a tolerance and a dependence on the drug or alcohol. The therapy needed may have to be more intense, too. These answers should lead you to conclude that the person really does need help before entering any long-term relationship with you.

Question 4. If the answer to this first part is yes, you are dealing with the Adult Child of an Alcoholic (ACOA). It has been discovered over the past twenty years that the alcoholic adversely affects seventeen other people on average. But the person who suffers most and often understands it least is the child. He or she is subjected to constant uncertainty, verbal and sometimes physical and sexual abuse—a chaotic world that leads them to learn secretive, evasive, and demeaning ways in order to survive. It tears away self-esteem and gives them an upside down view of the world.

There is a tremendous amount of damage that needs to be undone if that person is going to be able to handle life in a normal

manner, and especially life with you in a marriage. Their relationship with their parents will seem to be bizarre to someone who
hasn't grown up that way. They will have a strong tendency to
become alcoholics themselves or to spend much of their energy in
an extreme reaction to drinking, especially that of the alcoholic
parent, even if they drink themselves. They often have controlling
personalities, but just as often they are codependent rescuers who
fill their lives with chaos so that they can attempt to control life or
be rescued themselves. There may be lots of buried and expressed
anger that erupts at family events, and lots of over-compensation
and guilt. If this sounds like a pretty difficult thing to live with, it
really is. It is as baffling to the ACOA as it is to you; they don't
know why they react the way they do.

   If there is hope for you and this person to be happy together,
it lies in whether they have received help in dealing with the
damage or are willing to do so. They need counseling and/or a
recovery group geared for people who have the same problem. The
therapy may take quite awhile. If you plan on helping them through
it, you must be prepared for them to want to quit, and help them not
to give up. You will have to learn a lot about the ACOA syndrome
yourself and perhaps attend meetings with them. It is not easy. If
they got help in Alateen, did they stay with it long enough to do
some good? If the alcoholic parent got help, there is a likelihood
that things will be easier for the child, but the child needs his or her
own help.

   Also, you need to decide whether you want to go through the
effort and time it will take to see this person through the recovery
process. Again, don't feel like it is up to you to rescue this person.
You will want to salvage them. After all, they did not invite this
terrible upbringing. But they don't need excuses for their behavior,
or someone to rescue them from their problem. They need to deal
with it. They must do this process on their own, and any attempt to
rescue will hurt rather than help. All you can do is point them
toward the help they need and then wait to see whether they really
try to get it.

Question 5. If the answer is Yes, a lot depends on how they define recovered or recovering. In AA, they really mean the slogan "one day at a time." They don't refer to themselves as recovered, but only talk about how long they've remained sober. They know they can slip at any time. Although that is not the only approach to treatment, it seems to be the one that works the best.

But even in what are called managed recovery programs, in which the person is taught how to drink moderately and responsibly, a person isn't considered cured just because they went through the process. So if your prospective mate says they are cured and that they don't go to meetings any more, how long have they been sober? Are they kidding themselves, still drinking in an uncontrolled manner, or hiding their problem? If so, they are a poor choice for a mate, and they are far from cured. Remember, what they *do* is far more important than what they *say*. Do not overestimate your ability to change the alcoholic or endure life with such a person.

Questions 6, 7 and 8. These questions just help you to get a picture of how bad the problem is, and how it affects you and others. If you find you are embarrassed or uncomfortable when they drink or take drugs because of the way they treat you and others, you are definitely sensing a real problem. Ask yourself if you want to put up with that kind of behavior in a marriage. Do you want to be a golf or football widow while he goes out to get drunk with the boys? Do you want a life filled with excuses and broken promises caused by alcohol or drugs? If not, get them to treatment, or get out, or both. This marriage will be a real nightmare.

The recent death of comedian Phil Hartman and his wife was one of those tragic, seemingly senseless events that happen to people whom other people think have it made. Phil was respected and at the top of his profession, a nice guy with a beautiful wife and a million-dollar home in one of the nicest suburbs of Los Angeles. But his wife, Brynn, had battled cocaine and alcohol addictions for years. She had a huge hole in her self-esteem that two children, a high-profile marriage, and more luxury than most people ever see could not fill. She was in and out of rehab several times but never got the long-term help that she needed. Phil humored her, ignored her rages, bought her a gun when she felt insecure, and did most of the ineffective things people do who want to help an alcoholic but don't understand how.

He finally ran out of patience and loyalty. When she came home intoxicated (the autopsy showed a deadly mixture of cocaine, alcohol, and a tranquilizer) she accused him of unfaithfulness (a recurring theme of their arguments that was, at least at first, a fantasy on her part). Phil lost control and reportedly threatened to leave her and take the children (something you should never do to someone who is drinking and out of control). No one knows exactly what happened next, but apparently Brynn got the gun he had given her and shot him three times. In despair, she later turned the gun on herself, even though her young children were nearby.

A lot of lessons can be learned from this sad story, but the most important fact for you to remember is that Phil knew she had problems even before they were married. He thought he could beat the odds. He didn't get real help for himself or for her. His mistakes and hers cost both their lives. Don't let their story become your story. If you or your intended have a drug or alcohol problem, now is the time to get help, get out, or both.

So much for alcohol and drug problems and addictions. There are, of course, other addictions that pose major problems, such as gambling, eating, and sexual addictions. Often, they are related to alcohol and drug addictions or covered up by them. We'll screen for those elsewhere. But keep on, there is still hope out there.

Chapter 3

Respect Is the Bottom Line

Each one of you must love your wife as he loves himself,
and the wife must respect her husband.

Saint Paul, Ephesians 5:33

It doesn't get said often enough in marriage manuals or counseling materials, but respect is really a bottom-line issue in making a marriage work. If your mate is someone you can respect, and if they treat you with respect, you can overcome most of the obstacles life will throw at you, and work out differences you may have. Once one of you loses respect for the other, almost nothing will save the relationship. That is why infidelity, dishonesty, or violation of deeply held beliefs or promises so often results in divorce. But usually there are warning signs that can let you know whether a person respects himself or herself and you. Pay attention to them now and you can save yourself a lot of grief later.

Georgia and Dale had been married for twenty years. They had two sons. He was a successful banker, which conferred a certain amount of social prominence on his wife as well. He had a quick wit and a great story for any occasion. The two of them presided at clubs and social events. Both were considered community leaders. He had the reputation of being someone to whom you could go if you really needed help.

One day the bank examiners descended on the branch. A chilling discovery surfaced. Dale had been making improperly secured loans to people whom he knew needed help. He hadn't profited in any way from the transactions, but it was considered so serious an offense that he was fired from his position as president and became virtually unemployable in the banking industry. Friends rallied around him at first, but as time wore on he withdrew, became depressed and bitter, and let himself go. Georgia came to see me. She was ready to quit.

It wasn't so much that he had made the mistake and been fired, she said. He was trying to do something good and had done it the wrong way. But what had happened since had destroyed her respect for him. He had always been strong, confident, and optimistic. He was her shoulder to lean on when things got rough. But now he was drinking too much, had been laying around the house feeling sorry for himself, was irritable with her and their sons, and was refusing to see anyone. He seemed to be helpless. I pointed out that he was showing signs of real depression, but to her it was something more. He had stepped over a fine line that separated respect from disrespect. Had he not died suddenly of a heart attack, their marriage would have ended in divorce.

Since feeling respect is sometimes rather subjective; that is, you may respect someone because they are kind, or powerful, or courageous, or intelligent, or unfailingly courteous, or maybe a combination of all of those things, it is not easy to define. It is never easy to define a feeling in any case. But our feelings about someone are usually the result of actions they take, and we can decide if we respect those actions or not.

So the questions below are to help you sort out those feelings in certain areas and about certain actions. If you think of others, add them. You could start out by writing down the answers to the statement "I respect him or her because…" and then list the things they do that make you respect them. If you can get your prospective mate to write the same kind of list about you, you will be able to see what respect means to them. Is it the same thing to you?

Here are some questions to help you clarify how you feel:

1. Does he or she treat you with respect? (Include how he or she makes you feel, in public, in private, around their friends, your friends) *(Circle answers)*
    Always   Most of the time   Sometimes   Rarely   Never

2. Does he or she respect your saying "No":
    About places you don't want to go?   Yes   No
    About things you don't want to do?   Yes   No
    About sex?   Yes   No
    About seeing other people?   Yes   No

3. Does he or she respect themselves? Does their respect for themselves show in the following areas:
    Appearance (do they care what they look like?)   Yes   No
    How they treat their body   Yes   No
    How they treat their own things   Yes   No
    Is their word good?   Yes   No
    Do they work hard and do their best?   Yes   No
    Are they reckless, a daredevil?   Yes   No

4. Does he or she respect their parents? (Are they courteous to them or rude? Do they refer to them respectfully when they aren't there to hear?)   Yes   No   Don't know
    If he or she does not respect their parents, why not?
    If there are real resentments, have they been healed or are there still deep wounds?   Yes   No

5. Does he or she treat the following with respect:
    Peers (equals)?   Yes   Sometimes   No
    Waiters, salespeople in stores, hired help?
    Yes   Sometimes   No

People in authority, police, teachers, their boss?
Yes   Sometimes   No
Minorities?   Yes   Sometimes   No
Older people?   Yes   Sometimes   No

6.   Does he or she respect other people's property (including yours)?   Yes   No

7.   Are there any times when you feel that he or she is unfair, unjust, treats people wrongly, or cuts corners to avoid taking responsibility or paying his or her fair share?
Yes   No

Comments

Most of these questions are straightforward, and the bottom line is often how you feel about a certain action he or she has taken. But if the answers to these questions remind you of times you have been made to feel uncomfortable because of the way he or she did or wanted to do things, pay attention to those feelings! It is often some little thing that we saw in the beginning that tips us off to the character of a person we later find out to have been a con artist or crook. A little act of irresponsibility, a willingness to cheat, or cruelty to something or someone helpless can reveal a lot about how it will be to live with someone later on. One of the best things anyone can say about their mate is that they can always respect and depend on them.

Question 1. How does he or she make you feel when you are with them? Is it the same all the time, or is it different depending on whom they are trying to impress? Do you ever feel put down or demeaned because of things he or she says about you? Does he or she defend you if their friends put you down? If you don't feel respected most of the time, is this how you want it to be? Now is the time for a good talk, or to decide this is not the right person for you. If you go along with rudeness, unkindness, and disrespect, you are inviting further abuse. A sure sign of future problems with physical abuse is verbal abuse now. If you don't respect yourself enough not to put up with verbal abuse, how can you expect your intended to respect you?

Question 2. When you say no, does he or she listen? Do they respect your decision, or argue with it? Do they go along, but pout, or hassle you about it later? You have a right to say no about things that matter to you, and not be called a prude or a weirdo because of it. If you are not respected now, how will it be later? This is pretty clear-cut evidence on which to base a decision.

Question 3. There are probably other things that could be added to this list, but the bottom line—however you define it—is whether they respect themselves? If they do not, they will have a hard time respecting you or others. Poor self-esteem is at the root of many behavioral problems, and self-esteem is the one thing you cannot give someone else. The person who does not love or respect himself or herself can take all of the love you have to give and still come up empty, having drained you dry. It is not a pretty picture, and it makes for a very unhappy marriage. If you sense a basic disrespect, **get out while the getting is good.**

Question 4. A good sign of how a person will respect themselves and others is how well they respect their parents. There are parents who do not deserve respect because of abusive behavior, abandonment, etc. But most people who have dealt with their emotional scars in a healthy way do not trash their parents to their face or treat them rudely, no matter how bad they've been. If your potential mate is disrespectful to his parents, especially if there seems to be no particularly good reason, how will he or she be as a parent?

What will he or she be teaching your children by the way they treat their parents? How will they end up treating you? There may be a lot more at stake in the answer to this question than it first appears. If there is abuse in the background, and it hasn't been dealt with, that needs to be the top priority before you continue the relationship. Almost all adult child abusers were abused themselves as children. Since therapy to undo the damage from child abuse most probably means long-term counseling, decide now whether you want that in your future.

Question 5. How he or she treats others is a great clue to how they will treat you, and how you will end up feeling in social situations. There is nothing quite as embarrassing as being the spouse of someone who is rude or overbearing to waiters or salespeople. There is nothing quite as uncomfortable as hearing your mate run down other people, or be rude to others in your presence. Openly expressed racial slurs or demeaning comments will end up feeling like they reflect on you even though you didn't say them. You will be wondering why you ever picked this person for a mate in the first place—which is why you should think about it now. It won't improve just because you marry; in fact, it will undoubtedly get worse.

Marty and Karen would go to restaurants where she would seemingly always come up with some way to complain enough about the food to end up getting a free meal. At first it seemed cute. She would argue store clerks into taking back merchandise that was clearly used because she didn't want to pay for it. She always argued to get something thrown in for nothing on every deal. At first it seemed like she was just a sharp trader. But after two years of marriage it became apparent that she made a lifestyle out of creating a chaotic, combative moment every place they went. The abuse she heaped on her "inferiors" started being directed at her husband who "wouldn't stick up for her." Verbal abuse became physical abuse. The marriage ended in the most bewildering way possible. But Marty could have seen it coming had he paid attention to the clues.

Question 6. This can mean anything, from whether he or she takes things that don't belong to them, to misusing or abusing things that aren't theirs. If the answer is yes, this is something you should talk about now, as it will be a bigger problem the longer you have to live with it. Sometimes this is a sign that the person may have other major personality problems.

A girl whom I knew repeatedly bought dresses, wore them to parties, returned them the next day, and didn't think there was anything wrong with doing so. But later she revealed by her behavior that she didn't think there was anything wrong with cheating on her boyfriend or sleeping with almost anyone in pants. She had a problem with poor judgment, sex addiction, and was a classic codependent, the child of alcoholics. You may see only one sign. You may think that maybe they weren't taught any better, maybe they don't even know they do it. But disrespect for other people's property is a real character flaw that can lead to criminal behavior and legal problems. It is worth discussing now.

Question 7. This is a reflection question. What does the answer reveal about the character of your potential mate? If you can think of an event in which their behavior made you question their honesty, fairness, or ethics, do you know the whole situation, so that you are not leaping to a conclusion? If not, can you discuss it, or is he or she defensive? If his or her reasons are strange or evasive, don't disregard your instincts here. If it feels wrong, chances are it is. Do you want to be with someone who is unfair, unjust, or cuts corners? What could it lead to later on?

Sarah was an extremely bright and talented girl who I watched grow up to be a rebellious teenager. Her adoptive parents were mild mannered church people who had raised three other very calm girls. But she was a baffling challenge to them and everyone else. For some reason she liked to talk to me, though we often couldn't get past the wall that she used to fend off serious questions. She had a very strong conversion experience, which she tried to hold onto, but she couldn't seem to stay out of trouble. She would often say that it was no fun to be good all the time or that it felt good to be bad. She lied a lot, stole things, though not enough to get arrested, but finally drifted into drugs and sexual problems and ran away from home.

I never asked her the right question. Years later, after she had happily straightened out her life and undertaken missionary work, she finally told me that she had been raped as a child by a relative. When she tried to tell her family, they didn't believe her. She had done bad things because she had been made to feel that she was bad for lying. She concluded that she must have been bad for that to happen to her. Her reasoning was circular. Her acting out was to confirm or prove that she was as bad as everyone said. Which all goes to show that there can be some pretty deep issues churning under the surface of some seemingly small behavior problems.

Respect for you, respect for themselves, and respect for others are all important qualities in the person you are seeking to love and the person who will love you for a lifetime. Don't settle for anything less!

Press on! There are more good questions ahead in your search for a marriage that works.

Chapter 4

Money, Money, Money!

Money never made a man happy yet, nor will it. There is nothing in its nature to produce happiness. The more a man has, the more he wants, Instead of it filling a vacuum, it creates one. Better is little with the fear of the Lord, than great treasure, and trouble therewith.

Benjamin Franklin

An old friend of mine, a minister for over forty years, said that in all the time he had spent counseling people with marriage problems, the most common issues were money, sex, and the raising of children...in that order. I've found that to be true, too, although he would probably agree that while those are the problems presented, they are not necessarily the real problems. Nothing can make a problem worse than to have a money problem on top of it. And many a money problem is really about how we value money and what it does for us. If two people have very different ideas and values about money, it can cause problems in every aspect of their married life. The time to evaluate is before you are married.

Nate and Molly were always arguing over money, they said. As the two faced me across the desk, I sensed that this wasn't the only thing bothering them. The two were attractive: his blond and athletic good looks matching her cheerleader vitality. They seemed to be smarter than average and had good jobs. The problem, he said, was that he was working as hard as he felt he could, and going up the company ladder at a good rate. But she always wanted more money, and could spend it faster than he could make it. Every pay raise was spent before he got it.

Her side was that they had plenty of money, but that he insisted on knowing where every dime was going and balancing the budget every month. When she wanted to spend money on fixing up their house, he wouldn't let her use a credit card to do so. He wanted to put so much away in savings and retirement accounts that she felt there wasn't any money left to live well now. She also felt that he was so conservative that he wasn't going aggressively after the job openings that would pay more.

With a little probing, it became apparent that they came from very different backgrounds. His family had suffered some disastrous financial reversals early in his life and had struggled to make ends meet. He had concluded that he never wanted that to happen to him, and the only way to avoid that was to be extremely careful about credit and savings. Because he had heard the continuous family quarrels in which his mother berated his father for the recklessness that had caused their poverty (much of which was probably overstated), he concluded that the husband had to be the one to really take charge of finances and never let the family down.

Molly's family had always been comfortably well off. Her father had a good job, and her mother was a teacher. Both participated in financial decisions, and neither was particularly concerned to have a few debts owing. They didn't communicate any grave concerns about money to their children, but they didn't spoil them either. She had worked ever since high school. She had handled her finances well during and after college, where they had met.

The arguments about money were really as much about control as about finances. Nate was driven by a fear of failure to assume that he needed to control every spending move they made so that they would not end up like his parents. When Molly seemed to be so much less rigid about spending, it reminded him of his father. When she argued with him, it reminded him of his mother. All these unhappy reminders made him unable to deal on an adult basis with the realities of their situation. He turned out to be rather rigid about other things too, like sex, and when they might start a family. Molly felt stifled by his need to control things she was used to handling competently, and had nagged him about symptoms rather than dealing with the problem.

With some fairly long-term counseling, in which both gained insights about how their very different backgrounds had influenced their lives, Nate was eventually able to let go of his unreasonable fears and trust Molly enough to do joint budgeting and planning. Molly learned what triggered his fears and discovered new ways to communicate so that they could discuss choices rather than end up in an argument. As I said, money wasn't their only problem, but when they learned to deal constructively with finances, other areas improved also. It would have saved a lot of grief had they dealt with these differences before they got married.

The questions below should be part of any discussion you have about your future. As you listen to him or her and observe what you think money means to them, do a reality check. What he or she says is less important than what they do. Be aware that people's needs are always expanding, and tend to expand faster the more they have. If they say their needs are simple, ask what they mean by that. To some people, an adequate car is a Mercedes! That can be a problem if you are on an Escort budget. So here are some good questions:

1. How do *you* value money? What does it do for you? (***Check all that apply***)
    __ Having money makes me feel good
    __ Having money makes me feel secure
    __ Spending money makes me feel good
    __ Spending money makes me feel important

__ Saving money in the bank makes me feel in control

__ Saving money on a purchase makes me feel good or smart

__ Money is a necessity, but I don't need a lot to make me happy

__ Having money is a way that I know I'm successful.

__ I like to shop when money is no object

__ Money isn't everything, but it is way ahead of whatever is in second place

__ In order to have the things I want, I want to have a lot of money

__ I want the best for my family, more than I had growing up

__ I believe a penny saved is a penny earned

__ A lot of times it doesn't pay to try to save, or shop around

__ I think budgets are for losers

__ I like to plan ahead for spending on things I need

2. How does your prospective mate value money? What does it do for them?

__ Having money makes him or her feel good

__ Having money makes him or her feel secure

__ Spending money makes him or her feel good

__ Spending money makes him or her feel important

__ Saving money in the bank makes him or her feel in control

__ Saving money on a purchase makes him or her feel good or smart

__ Money is a necessity, but he or she doesn't need a lot to make them happy

__ Having money is a way that he or she knows they are successful.

__ He or she likes to shop when money is no object

__ Money isn't everything, but it is way ahead of whatever is in second place

__ In order to have the things he or she wants they want to have a lot of money

__ He or she says, "I want the best for my family, more than I had growing up."
__ He or she says, "A penny saved is a penny earned."
__ He or she says, "A lot of times it doesn't pay to try to save, or shop around."
__ He or she thinks, "Budgets are for losers."
__ He or she likes to plan ahead for spending on things they need

3. How much money would you say it would take for you to be living the way you want to live?
_____ (per year)
How much would your prospective mate say?
_____ (per year)
If that means both of you working, are you both willing to do so?   How long?

4. Describe you and your potential mate in the following terms: *(Circle all that apply)*

YOU	POTENTIAL MATE
Spender	Spender
Saver	Saver
Giver	Giver
Taker	Taker
Miser	Miser
Generous	Generous
Thrifty	Thrifty
Careless	Careless
Careful	Careful
Extremely Cautious	Extremely Cautious

5. Does he or she use money to buy affection, to get out of trouble, to substitute for thoughtfulness or love?
Yes   No   Maybe

6. If it came to choosing to spend money on something you want, or something he or she wants, who would he or she spend it on? _____
    Who would you spend it on? _____

7. Has he or she had credit problems or other money problems? Yes   No
    Are they cleared up, or will you have to live with them? Yes   No

8. Does he or she like to gamble?   Never   Rarely   Often   Regularly
    If yes, does he or she risk large amounts?   Yes   No

9. Does he or she have an expensive hobby or sport they participate in regularly? _____
    Would they be willing to give it up to make ends meet? Yes   No

Comments

These question are attempting to reveal attitudes and values that will either allow you to work well together or cause major problems for you. There are other questions you might like to ask as you discuss how you would handle financial decisions, like who will be in charge of the finances in your home, who will handle the checkbook, and how you will make a decision when you have two needs and money to meet just one. But those kinds of questions can be resolved if both of you have compatible ideas about spending, saving, and managing money. If you have really basic differences in attitudes, they can't be resolved easily. Sometimes they can't be resolved at all. Since a lot of our attitudes come from early childhood, they are not easily changed.

Question 1 and 2 Look at the two lists. Are the answers similar or not? Does either of you tend to have extremely opposite ideas from the other? Don't minimize the importance of differences at this point. How each of you feels about money and what it does for you will determine how you will make the daily financial decisions that affect your long-term economic well being. If one of you likes to plan out expenses while the other thinks budgets are for losers, one of you will spend what the other has planned for something else. You will conclude that the other person doesn't love you enough to do things the "right" way, that they're irresponsible, too uptight, etc. This is a basic incompatibility. This is also ammunition for a major fight that will probably recur for as long as the marriage lasts.

Note that what money signifies is extremely important. If having money or spending it spells self-worth, success, or happiness for either one of you, it will become the prime motivator for your life. You or your potential mate will do whatever it takes to get more of it. It will determine whether one puts his or her job, possessions, financial security, or status ahead of family or anything else. Money can become an addiction. Workaholics are no fun to live with. Neither are spendthrifts. So how healthy are your attitudes and how healthy are his or hers? How opposite are they? If you sense major differences, this could be a real problem for your marriage. You will need to discuss these differences, preferably with a counselor or your minister, priest, or rabbi, before you marry.

Question 3. This is a reality check. How close are your answers? The U.S. Government defines the poverty level as at or below $20,000 a year for a family of three, but how much do you think you need? If it takes more than one of you working to make that amount, are you both willing to work? If not, what is the answer? If one of you is willing to work for awhile until you start a family, how will you handle the loss of income when you do? These are really good questions to talk about now rather than later. And make sure the answers are truthful. A person might say they are willing to work, but if their real dream is to stay home and be a parent and homemaker, they will soon be pressuring you to make more money so they can quit and stay home. The argument will seem to be about money, but it is really about expectations that should have been made clear before you were married.

It is a very good idea to get a little family history. Did his or her parents both work? How did he or she feel about that? Did their mother force the issue and have children before they were really ready so that she could stay home? Or did Dad make her stay home and not work when she wanted a career? Some of these family histories have an uncanny way of repeating themselves in your family. Beware, especially if there was some deceit involved, or if there is some unhappiness or a history of alcohol problems in that family.

Question 4. Again, this is a check for compatibility. The words are opposites, some more extremely opposite than others. If you come out as a spender, generous, and careless, and your mate comes out as a miser, a taker, and extremely cautious, major conflict will be inevitable. But words like saver, generous, giver, thrifty, and careful are not as extreme. They imply that while you may not be exactly alike, there is room for compromise. You can deal with differences, but the more extreme they are the more difficult that will become. Counseling can help, provided you both agree to it and stick with it. But if you encounter extreme differences, and one of you is not willing to talk about them or change, this may not be the right match for you.

Question 5. This is a very revealing question. If the answer is yes, or maybe, you are dealing with a problem that is deeper than money. The person who has learned to substitute money for affection will have great difficulty relating to you or to your children. Sometimes they will appear to be generous, always giving gifts, or being very fair about seeing that everyone gets treated equally. But if you get the feeling that you would rather have intimacy or affection than a present, pay attention to those feelings.

This may be the only way a person learned to show or receive affection from a parent who had difficulty expressing emotions. It most often is a learned behavior, but it is learned from someone who has a problem with intimacy. Marriage to such a person is a very lonely ordeal. Again, take a look at his or her family.

Question 6. The answers speak for themselves. While the question is about spending, it really reveals character. Be honest—how much is either one of you willing to sacrifice to make the other happy? Actions speak more loudly than words. Selfishness is not something that improves with age nor is it automatically cured by marriage. There may be many times when you will need to put the other person first and sacrifice some of your own needs for the sake of the other. That is really what love is all about. But it needs to be a two-way street. If one of you does all the giving while the other does all the taking, one will feel cheated while the other will accumulate guilt, which they will act out in many unhealthy ways.

If you feel that your intended would not choose to spend on you rather than on themselves, it is likely that you are sensing a basic character flaw. It is not the sort of thing that is cured by anything short of a real religious or personality conversion. You can pray, but be prepared to cross this person off your list.

Question 7. If you don't know, now is a good time to ask. If you or your prospective mate has a history of credit problems, or has bad credit, neither of you should expect the other to rescue them. If the problems are the result of a divorce or business failure, have they been dealt with through bankruptcy, consumer credit counseling, or some other channel? Know where you stand before you find someone else's problems becoming your own. Your good credit history can be ruined by your spouse's bad one unless you keep all accounts separate. Be aware that people *do* marry people in order to get their money or cure their own financial problems. Don't be their victim! It is a bad sign if your prospective mate is evasive about money, or what they do to make it. They also could be covering up for criminal behavior.

Question 8. Gambling can be as serious an addiction as alcohol and drugs. The proliferation of casinos and other forms of legalized gambling have resulted in a much higher number of people who have serious financial and legal problems. Calls to the Gambling Addiction hotline in Oregon rose by seventy percent last year (1997). The social consequences range from family breakup, mental breakdown, and divorce to embezzlement and fraud as people try to get out of their gambling debts.

Buying an occasional lottery ticket or playing a few games at a casino on a vacation is not serious gambling. But if someone is constantly looking for the day that he will win the big one, or is starting to borrow in order to gamble or to pay off gambling debts, they are in trouble and need help. If they are postponing what they realistically need to do at work in order to place bets or sneak off to the track, they are in need of help. Gamblers Anonymous or similar programs can help—you can't. Unless you are a glutton for the peculiar form of punishment a gambler's spouse has to take, cross this person off your list unless they get help now and are willing to stick with it. If you are not sure your intended has a problem, call Gamblers Anonymous and describe their behavior. They can spot it quickly.

Question 9. This is usually a guy problem, unless she is into horses, golf, or shopping as a hobby. It is a serious question though. Many an unhappy wife plays second fiddle to some expensive toy or recreation. I once knew a lady whose entire house, including the living and dining room, was taken over by spare parts for classic cars that her husband was always fixing. She was never able to have anyone in her home socially, and it was obvious from her clothes where the familys income went. She ended up pretty much raising her daughter alone, too, as hubby could never get his head out from under the hood. Would this be you? If you see a problem here, and it is not a hobby you share or want to share, now is a good time to reconsider this relationship.

When George and Sheila came to talk about their problems, I wasn't too surprised that they started with money. They had married as students and had scraped by with help from parents. She had worked and finished her undergraduate degree first while he worked part-time and earned his degree plus an additional year needed for accreditation. While she had advanced rapidly at her company, he had a slow time getting started in a very competitive field. But they had finally just about caught up with their debts when he landed his first real job.

But by then, Sheila was tired of the apartment life they had been living and decided they needed a house. By stretching, and with help from parents, they managed to get a very nice, small home in a good neighborhood. Of course, they needed furniture, the best they could get. A new car was next, then a second car, a small boat, yard equipment, and deck furniture. Suddenly they found themselves swimming in debt. George had tried to rein her in but found that she became so verbally and even physically abusive when he did so that he stopped trying.

Could this marriage be saved? Possibly. Had they sought help earlier they would have understood that money meant very different things to each of them. To George, money was to be used carefully so that they could live comfortably within their means and satisfy wants as they could afford them. Large debts made him uncomfortable and, since she often implied that he was not as successful as she was, made him feel like a failure.

To Sheila, money was a sign that she had escaped the confusing and somewhat poverty-stricken life she had known as a child. Her father had doled out money instead of the affection he could not give, but there wasn't enough to make his family feel good about their home and circumstances. He was also a drinker and sometimes physically abusive, even though they presented a happy (if hypocritical) front to their community and church. Money represented affection, comfort, security, and escape. And all of those were infinitely expanding needs. The more she had, the more she wanted, and if George couldn't give them to her he was expendable, or at least beratable.

Sheila was an Adult Child of an Alcoholic (see Chapter 2), very much in denial and very codependent. She was unable to deal with the demons that were driving her, and succeeded only in driving George out of her life. The result was divorce, bankruptcy, and sheer misery. Money wasn't their only problem, but it made everything else even worse. A few more questions asked before this marriage might have warned them to get help or call it off.

So much for the money questions. Now on to something everybody seems to talk about, but without much agreement and often much confusion. How does your intended do in the sex department? Turn the page.

Chapter 5

Sex, Sex, Sex!

Civilized people can never satisfy their sexual instinct without love.

Bertrand Russell

Sex is never an emergency.

Dr. Elaine Pierson

Sex is undoubtedly the most over-discussed topic in the media. Sex is used to sell everything from apple juice to underwear, and is flaunted in just about every way possible on our big and little screens. Freud has triumphed. This is no longer the Victorian era, when no one talked about sex in public. Today it is talked about so much we wish it would stop. But that hasn't diminished it as a problem area for many marriages. In fact, while the mechanics of sex are better understood and discussed more than ever before, the problems are as old as time.

Phyllis and Frank were what everyone described as a fun couple. She was vivacious, good looking for her thirty-five-something age, and the mother of two knockout daughters. Frank was handsome, successful, and outgoing. We'd had a small group course on marriage and some of the things that were said led me to believe that all was not as it looked on the surface in their marriage. Nervous laughter and some barbs about the infrequency of sex after the honeymoon had worn off were hints of problems. But I was unprepared for the day that Frank walked in to ask me if I thought he was a really immoral man.

I asked him why he thought I would feel like that, and he began to tell me that he had been having dreams and fantasies about falling in love with his oldest teenage daughter. His company had hired her as a summer intern, and as he saw her constantly in the office, he found he was having distinctly un-fatherly feelings for her. He hadn't acted on any of these impulses, and he felt guilty for even thinking about her this way, but he was afraid of where this might lead.

As we talked, he confessed to having had similar fantasies about a young clerk who had worked in his office a year previously. Again, he hadn't acted on his impulses, though she was something of a flirt, and she had moved away. But as he described her, he realized that she was a dead ringer for his daughter, who was herself nearly a carbon copy of her mother. What was going on?

With some precautions taken so that he was not around his daughter at work so much, we began a series of counseling sessions for Frank and Phyllis. Frank, it turned out, was having something of a midlife crisis: He felt like he was at a dead end in his work, and was feeling less than fulfilled in his marriage. Phyllis was vaguely unhappy, worried that she was not as attractive as she had been (she knew about the clerk and sensed that she was a rival), and was frankly dissatisfied that their sex life was virtually nonexistent.

Their problems had started early on in their marriage. They had been passionately attracted to each other in high school (he was a year older), and after his first year in college they got married because she became pregnant. (You would be amazed at how many stories of marital difficulties start out that way!) He finished school and she started college classes, which were interrupted by a second pregnancy. The second birth was difficult, and postnatal recovery kept her from wanting sex for some time. He felt guilty for having caused her to suffer and for having stopped her schooling, but rather than deal with these feelings, they simply did not talk about them.

When Phyllis finally felt ready to resume sexual relations, Frank was so afraid of hurting her that he couldn't perform very well, and her tendency to sarcasm wounded him enough that he avoided sex entirely. They let things drift without getting help. The distractions of work, parenting, and several moves had kept them from dealing with the marital problems they felt but didn't talk about.

Counseling helped. Frank discovered that his fantasies were really about the Phyllis he had known before they had married and had problems. He still loved her, and they needed to talk about the fears that were separating them in order to rekindle the romance in their marriage. Phyllis was relieved to find out that he was still attracted to her, and learned how to convey her feelings without putting him down or turning him off. Once they got their marriage and sex life back on track, Frank was able to make a career move that made him happier at work. The last picture I saw of them was as a beaming Father and Mother of the Bride presiding at their oldest daughter's wedding.

When sex is a problem in a marriage, it often is not the whole problem, and the mechanics aren't usually the main issue. Attitudes, values, and feelings have much more to do with sex than the act of sexual intercourse itself. Although our popular culture has confused the terms, love and sex are not the same thing. And sex without love is not what most of us want. Nor do we want to end up with someone who has real sexual hang-ups or deviant behaviors. If you are heterosexual you don't want to marry a homosexual. You do want someone who will be faithful.

Unfortunately, some of these things are difficult to screen out. But if you feel that something isn't quite right, don't ignore those feelings. Ask some hard questions and do some investigation. You don't have to move in together or have intercourse to find out, either. Sex is not an emergency! No one ever died from not having sex, but plenty are dying from AIDS and other diseases. You do have to pay attention and not let your judgment get clouded by thinking things will change or get better after marriage.

Here are some questions that can help:

1.   Which of these statements describe your attitudes or values? *(Check all that apply)*
__ I like sex any time, anywhere, with anyone I can get it
__ I think sex belongs only in a marriage or a committed relationship
__ I like sex with people of the same sex as well as the opposite sex
__ I think marriage shouldn't mean you always have to be faithful
__ I don't think sex is too important in a marriage as long we're happy
__ I like to watch X-rated films or other people having sex
__ I think sex is something really private. I don't even like these questions
__ I think any kind of sex is OK as long as both people feel comfortable
__ I think sex is kind of dirty
__ Sex is good if I feel good when I'm done
__ Sex is good if we both feel fulfilled when we're done
__ I'm a virgin, I don't know much about sex
__ I'm pretty experienced, but I don't want my mate to be
__ My mate needs to be sexy
__ Sex is sinful; I try not to think about it too much
__ I think kindness and tenderness are more important than sex
__ Sometimes I wonder if I like people of my own sex better than the other
__ The best jokes are dirty jokes
__ If my mate likes to look at pornography, thats OK with me
__ I like to dress up as a person of the opposite sex

__ If my mate liked looking at pictures of children having sex it would bother me

__ If my mate liked to dress as a person of the opposite sex it would bother me

2. Which of the following statements describe **your potential mate's** attitudes or values? *(Check all that apply)*

__ He or she likes sex any time, anywhere, with anyone they can get it

__ He or she thinks sex belongs only in a marriage or a committed relationship

__ He or she likes sex with people of the same sex as well as the opposite sex

__ He or she thinks marriage shouldn't mean you always have to be faithful

__ He or she doesn't think sex is too important in a marriage as long we're happy

__ He or she likes to watch X-rated films or other people having sex

__ He or she thinks sex is something really private, won't discuss it

__ He or she thinks any kind of sex is OK as long as both people feel comfortable

__ He or she thinks sex is kind of dirty

__ He or she feels that, "Sex is good if I feel good when I'm done."

__ He or she feels that, "Sex is good if we both feel fulfilled when we're done."

__ He or she is a virgin, doesn't know much about sex

__ He or she is pretty experienced, but doesn't want me to be

__ He or she needs me to be sexy if they are going to be interested

__ He or she says, "Sex is sinful, I try not to think about it too much."

__ He or she says, "I think kindness and tenderness are more important than sex."

__ He or she has had homosexual relationships
__ He or she thinks the best jokes are dirty jokes
__ He or she says, "If my mate likes to look at pornography thats OK with me."
__ He or she likes to dress up as a person of the opposite sex
__ If I liked looking at pictures of children having sex it would bother him or her
__ If I liked to dress up as a person of the opposite sex it would bother him or her

3. Does he or she taunt you with stories about old flames or conquests?   Never   Often   Sometimes

4. Does he or she talk about sex easily?   Yes   No

5. Has he or she ever been sexually abused?   Yes   No
    If yes, have they had counseling and long-term help?
    Yes   No   Don't Know

6. What is his or her parents' marriage like? *(Check all that apply)*
    __ Happy
    __ Average, not happy or unhappy
    __ Unhappy
    __ Divorced
    __ Divorced and remarried, now happy
    __ Divorced and remarried more than once
    __ Father was unfaithful, resulting in divorce
    __ Father unfaithful, but marriage continues
    __ Mother unfaithful, resulting in divorce
    __ Mother unfaithful, marriage continues

7. Does he or she pressure you about having sex?   Yes   No
    Has he or she ever forced you to have sex when you didn't want to?   Yes   No

8. Does he or she practice safe sex (if sexually active)?
   Yes   No   Hasn't in past

Comments

The questions have two purposes. One is to help you focus on your own attitudes and values, and to help you contrast them with those of your intended mate's. The other is to screen for some potentially serious sexual dysfunction or problem that could cause difficulties later on. Some of them require you to delve into your potential mate's family history, but usually you can get this information by simply asking what his or her family is like and just listening carefully.

Question 1 and 2. What are your values and what are your prospective mate's? What are you comfortable with, and what is he or she comfortable with that you are not? Where are the danger signals? If either one of you agrees with the first statement, that they like sex with anyone, anytime, anywhere, the other had better agree too, or one of you will be miserable. But in fact, the person who says this is not ready to settle down and devote himself or herself to one person. The same is true of the person who says that marriage shouldn't mean you have to be faithful. If your intended mate says this, *believe that he or she means it.* You won't change them no matter how hard you try to be a good husband or wife, or try to be sexier than anyone else out there. Marriage to an unfaithful partner is the stuff tragic romance novels are made of, but is that what you want?

The so-called open marriage works for very few people. Question 6 deals with family history in more depth, but you should know that if a father is unfaithful, his sons are very apt to be womanizers as well, especially if the mother allows him to get away with it. The Kennedys are a great case study. It is also true that daughters will pick up many messages from mothers who are unfaithful. At the least, they will be very reluctant to trust anyone.

Daughters whose fathers are unfaithful may assume that that kind of marriage is normal and will often make the mistake of marrying a womanizer themselves. Do you want that kind of marriage? What do you want your children to learn from your marriage?

The statement about having sex with others of the opposite sex can help you screen out potentially homosexual partners. Even if people call themselves switch hitters, or say they were just experimenting, you could be and most probably are dealing with someone whose own sexual identity is weak. You are not going to be that person's savior. Finding someone of the opposite sex who makes their other desires go away does not cure homosexuals. They need counseling and help to find out who they are, and what sexual identity they will assume. In the meantime, do you want to be exposing yourself to someone who is indulging in the most dangerous kinds of sexual activity, not knowing if they practice safe sex or not? It only takes once to get AIDS. (This is a good time to remind you that you can get AIDS from anyone—straight, gay, or switch hitter—who is promiscuous and does not use protection.)

The real difficulty in determining if your partner is homosexual or not is that they may not be sure themselves and may be attempting to hide it. Many women and men have said they had no clue that their mate was gay. Some had children, and marriages that lasted several years. However, many would say when pressed that they just thought that he or she wasn't very interested in sex, or that they thought that it was nice that he didn't push about sex before marriage, that he was just a "real gentleman," etc. After marriage they simply assumed the person just wasn't too interested in sex, assumed that it was normal, and since other people seemed to have the same experience of a lessening of desire after marriage, just dismissed their feelings about this not being normal.

To me, this is an important clue. If your prospective mate isn't crazy about you, isn't often wanting to kiss you, snuggle, or even push things with you (you can always say no!) it may not be that they are just too much of a gentleman or a lady, it may be that they have ambivalent feelings. There should be some passion in your relationship, and it should be there long after you are married. (Of course, withdrawal from sex after marriage may also be a sign of a heterosexual affair, emerging memories of sexual abuse, or sexual addiction. It is not necessarily a sign of age—people are capable of having active sex lives into their 90s—but it is always a sign that the marriage is in trouble.) The worst thing that happens in a relationship that turns out to have been with a homosexual is that the person who isn't gay ends up blaming themselves ("I should have known," "I guess I wasn't sexy enough," etc.). It is not your fault that they are the way they are.

Pay attention to your feelings. If something doesn't feel right, maybe it isn't. Also pay attention to what others say. If they say something like, "I always thought he or she wasn't interested in boys/girls," or, "I thought he/she would never get married, he/she just wasn't interested," maybe they are telling you something important. If their best friend of the same sex seems to be more than just a friend, investigate. He or she may be the nicest, kindest, most artistic, or intellectually stimulating person you know, but will they be a good husband or wife? There is usually a clue.

There are two or three statements having to do with pornography. The point is to identify what you are comfortable with, and what you are not. If you aren't comfortable with it and he or she is, this will probably crop up as a source of conflict later. In general, in spite of its label as "adult" material, people who are really into pornography are indulging in rather immature or unrealistic sexual fantasies, and often have poor sexual identification or self-confidence. Be aware that pornography can become addictive, and it breeds an appetite for more and worse forms the longer one watches it.

If you enjoy watching X-rated movies together, and find them sexually stimulating together, then you may be operating in a normal way for you. Obviously, if both of you are repulsed by it and do not enjoy it, that is quite normal, too. If your potential mate has to have pornography to get aroused rather than being aroused by you, or if he or she enjoys this as their way of sexual gratification without you, that is quite a different matter. If he/she (usually) enjoys child pornography, watch out. Usually this is a good sign of sexual dysfunction, and is often the sign of a potential or actual child molester. If he/she watches homosexual pornography, this is a good sign that he/she is gay or tending toward homosexuality.

Some of the other statements deal with behavior that might or might not bother you. Some people like to cross-dress. This may be harmless, but if it bothers you and there are other signs that the person is not really comfortable with who he or she is, it could be a warning sign that this relationship is not for you. The same is true of dirty jokes. Some are funny, some are cruel or demeaning, and some are so gross you might be sickened. If the person says things or does things that offend or sicken you, do you want to be around them for the rest of your life?

Some of the statements define how considerate or how selfish the person is about sex. If he or she feels that sex is good if they get what they want, whether you feel satisfied or not, they are probably going to be self-centered in other ways too. If they are not considerate of your likes and dislikes, sex will be uncomfortable for you, for sure. If they are pretty experienced but want you to be a virgin, what kind of double standard does that represent? If you are required to be sexy in order to earn his or her love, you are always going to be looking over your shoulder to see if someone sexier is in the wings. Love implies acceptance. You may not be Mr. or Mrs. Universe, but they ought to love you for who you are. If he or she thinks you're sexy, that's all that matters.

Finally, there are a couple of attitude-screening statements to which you should pay particular attention. If either one of you feels that sex is dirty or particularly sinful, you will have a hard time having a normal sex life. Stop right now, and get some counseling from a counselor that is linked with your church, synagogue, or faith community. If they are worth their salt, they will tell you that no major religion regards sex itself as sinful. Misuse of sex or sex outside marriage may be regarded as sinful, but not sex per se. If one of you has picked up this attitude from your parents, you need to get help to understand or undo that attitude. If this is some kind of official teaching of your or your prospective mate's religious group, you may be dealing with a cult or a very narrow sect. You will probably not want to get more deeply involved with them. Cults often have bizarre attitudes about sex, which signal other major problems too. (See Chapter 11)

Question 3. The answer to this question is, hopefully, never. This is a form of torture to which no mate should be subjected. It is the fastest way to a big blowup I can imagine, and it is lethal ammunition if used in an argument. Comparisons to past flames or conquests are not something anyone can fight against, and they erode self-confidence to the point that a person feels they cannot compete. If your prospective mate does this, ask yourself why? Better yet, ask them why, and if they aren't willing to stop doing it, cross them off your list.

Occasionally, I run across a peculiar form of this problem that is sheer dynamite. A young man and his bride got to their honeymoon suite in St. Croix, all set to enjoy their first night as man and wife. In the middle of their lovemaking, she began calling out the name of a former flame whom he knew about and had assumed she was over. As you can imagine, the honeymoon was pretty much over. Thousands of dollars and beautiful scenery could not erase the damage. The moral: If you or your intended are still emotionally attached to someone else, give yourself enough time to make sure you aren't choosing someone on the rebound, and then vow to never mention the other person again.

Question 4. Some people don't find it easy to talk about sex. If he or she has a problem, first ask yourself if it is because you come across as judgmental, aggressive, sarcastic, or crude. You might ask them if you don't know. But at some point you are going to have to be able to talk about sex openly so that you will be able to know what makes each of you feel best. One thing you might do is just to suggest that they answer this set of questions. Make a game of it and compare answers. This could and should lead to a pretty open exchange.

It is important to know that the most important sexual organ is the brain, which is stimulated by words, visual images, and physical sensations. Men tend to be excited visually more than women. Tender words, touch, and shared feelings are extremely important to women. So if your communication about sex is clumsy or simply physical, you will not be able to communicate effectively.

Question 5. If he or she admits to being sexually abused as a child or raped as an adult, the second half of this question is extremely important. Sexual abuse leaves tremendous scars. If they have not received long-term help, they need to get it now. If it was abuse by a parent, the problem is even more devastating. If one parent was in denial and abetted the abuse by the other, you will be seeing a lot of rage, sexual dysfunction, and some nearly irreconcilable difficulties with their family. Abuse often produces codependency.

You cannot heal this by yourself; the aftermath of such abuse requires professional help. Getting help should be your top priority. Put any marriage plans on hold. Plan on long-term help and some ups and downs. You can be supportive, but be aware that the person has a lot of demons to exorcise, and it takes a long time to get over.

If you are puzzled by the person's sometimes-childish behavior, most therapists now treat the patient as if their emotional growth was arrested at the time the traumatic events occurred. They have to revisit that age and then be helped to grow up past the events in their life that caused all the pain. This is a job for a pastoral psychotherapist or clinical psychotherapist, not a psychologist. There is hope for the person, but they have to get help.

Question 6. While your marriage will be your own unique creation, and no two are exactly alike, your odds of being happy are much better if your parents' marriage was happy. This is because you will tend to model your marriage around the only operating model you saw personally. This means, unfortunately, that you will do so whether the model was good or bad. If you or your intended mate experienced more than one marriage, one good, one not so good, you may have learned a lot about what you want. But you may also have learned distrust, disappointment, how to hide feelings from one parent or the other, and sexual patterns that may not be helpful.

The scale ranges from the happiest to the unhappiest patterns. Cases in which one or both parents were unfaithful but the marriage remained intact might be cases in which both parties learned their lessons and put the marriage back together without recurring problems. But if there is a continuing problem of unfaithfulness, and the marriage exists because it is too difficult for one or the other to get out, then you can bet the children of that marriage have some king-size resentments and patterns to overcome. If the parents retaliated by having their own affairs, or punished one another by flaunting or withholding sex, the child will more than likely follow these patterns.

The sins of the fathers and mothers do seem to be visited on the children of such families. How this will work out in your marriage needs to be something you really discuss. You will need to draw the line and say what you expect in the way of faithfulness and commitment. If he or she doesn't see it that way because of the way they were raised (or more importantly, if they agree with your demand for faithfulness, but already show signs of unfaithful behavior), **now is the time to get out.**

Question 7. There is a difference between pressuring you and forcing you. A healthy interest in sex may result in pressure, but as long as you can say no and have the other person respect that, you are probably dealing with a normal person. *When someone forces you to have sex when you don't want to, that is rape.* Although it is more usual for males to rape females, there are cases of females forcing males to have sex as well.

You should never have to feel degraded or used, or forced to have sex. If you do, this is not a good relationship. Get out now before it becomes more abusive. The longer you stay, the worse it will get, and the harder it will be to leave. Spiritually speaking, the abuser becomes a god to the victim—they can't live without them. The sad story of abusive relationships is that they so befuddle the victim that they end up going back to the abuser until they are killed or until their children are threatened and they finally have that reason to get out. It is an awful situation, made worse by the fact that it's extremely hard to cure an abusive person. If you have been forced, **get out and get help now!**

Question 8. If you don't know the answer to this question, find out. If your prospective mate hasn't protected himself or herself in the past and you are sexually active with them, you are running some very heavy risks. Sexually transmitted diseases are no joke, and they can be fatal. If they don't care enough about you to protect you, why do you want to be with them?

You may have noticed that I haven't dealt with what is called kinky sex, rough sex, sadomasochism, drug-aided sex, or sex with multiple partners. Every one of these forms of sex involves the risk of injury or death. If someone asks you to participate in any of these forms of sex, they are asking you to do two things. The first is to risk your life for their pleasure. Your well being is not as important to them as their gratification. By definition, they do not love you as they love themselves. The second is that they are asking you to be a sex object rather than a human being with value and feelings. This is not love, it is satisfaction of their need to dominate, use someone, or degrade themselves. Such a person is not a good person for you to marry in any case. They do not love you, and you won't love them or yourself if you allow yourself to be used. If your intended pressures you to do any of these things, cross them off your list right now.

Well, a book could be written just about sex and marriage, and in fact there are some very good books available on this very topic, which I have listed in the bibliography. You deserve a happy and sexually satisfying marriage, and your mate does too. Finding the right partner is not a matter of sexual experimentation or living together before marriage. If you pay attention to the information they tell you every day, in conversation and in their actions, you can avoid making mistakes and can find someone who will be fun to live with for a lifetime.

Chapter 6

But What About the Children?

A happy family is but an earlier Heaven.

Sir John Bowring

Billy was in trouble again. He had skipped school and been caught stealing cigarettes from a local pharmacy. He probably thought they were candies; after all, he was only seven. His four-year-old sister was already rated a holy terror in our nursery school. Since Billy's "crime" involved a controlled product, police had intervened. His parents had been told to get counseling and had chosen to see me. They didn't say so, but I figured they thought I'd be easier on them than a Family Services "shrink."

It didn't take long to find out where the problem lay. Cindy, the mother, had run away from home in the last heady days of the anti-war movement. Her home life had been chaotic and abusive. She could remember hiding during her father's drunken rages, and crying silently as he took it out on her brother, who hadn't moved quickly enough. She vowed that, if she ever had children, she would never strike them or even raise her voice in anger. Somehow she got her life together, got some schooling, and met Marty at the place she worked. He was kind, considerate, and came from a nice family that didn't ask a lot of questions and accepted her into the fold.

They got married, but among the many things they didn't talk about was how they would raise the children, if they had any. Marty was easygoing and came from a family where Mom did most of the disciplining, but where Dad was the final arbiter who didn't hesitate to back her up with a spanking, if necessary. It had been a happy home and their way had worked well for the four children.

Marty had a busy job, requiring longer than average hours. When the children were little, he assumed that Cindy was managing them. He often didn't see them until after they were in bed. Some children are relatively easy to raise; some are what are termed strong-willed children. As luck would have it, Billy and Heather were the kind who challenged every limit and tested their parents to the utmost. Cindy's principle of lowered-voice discipline and no spanking might have worked with some children, but not these two. When challenged, she gave in to keep the peace, not realizing that she was creating more trouble down the line.

When Marty finally realized that there was a problem, he decided to step in and demand that the children either obey or face a spanking. He was unprepared for the hysterical reaction he got from Cindy, who threw herself between him and the children to keep him from touching them. Baffled, he retreated. Finding that discipline was something they couldn't discuss rationally, he told her it was up to her.

I wish I could tell you that this couple solved their problems through counseling. Perhaps they could have had they stayed longer with the counselor to whom I referred them. But both children got into more trouble, and Cindy wasn't able to deal rationally with the idea of discipline. Marty finally left. He said he didn't like the children well enough to fight for custody, so Cindy was left to raise them alone. I hesitate to think what they became like as teenagers and adults.

Children end up being the focus of a lot of marital problems. Although the best of children can cause heartache and struggles for parents, they usually aren't the problem themselves. Problems arise when people become parents who can't agree on when to have children, where and how to raise them, or whether they really want children at all. There are many good books on parenting, and they have many good ideas. All agree that parenting works best when both parents are involved and when both agree on basic things like discipline, rules, and communication. Since I am not writing a book on parenting here, I will list a few good books in the Bibliography. But there are issues you and your prospective mate ought to talk about before you are married, and the more you talk now, the more likely you will be able to avoid conflict later on.

If you want to have children, then you need a person who really wants to have children too, someone who wants the responsibility of raising them with you. It has now been documented rather extensively that children of two-parent homes do better in life than those who are raised by a single parent. This is not to disparage the efforts or the struggles that single parents go through because a spouse dies or leaves. There are heroic success stories that shine above the failures. But many single-parent situations could have been avoided by doing what you are doing now…asking good questions before you marry. Here are some to get you off on the right foot.

As is true of all the questions in this book, you need to supplement the answers you get from your prospective mate with observations of how they actually behave. Your intended may be very good at telling you exactly what he or she knows you want to hear. So observe how they really act around children. Do they really like children, and do children like them? Are they more like a kid themselves, or do they act in such a way that children look up to them? What kind of parent will they be?

1. Do you want to have children?   Yes   No
    Why or why not?

    What does having a child or children mean to you?

2.   Does he or she want to have children?   Yes   No
       Why or why not?

       What does having a child or children mean to him or her?

3.   How many children would you like to have?
       How many would he or she like to have?
       If your responses are different, what do you think he or she
       is really saying?

4.   When do you want to have children?
       When does he or she want to have children?
       If your responses are different, are the two of you willing to
       compromise on this?

5.   What do you see as the sacrifices necessary for raising
       children?

       What does he or she see as the sacrifices necessary for
       raising children?

6.   What part do you expect your prospective mate to play in
       child raising and care?
       What part does he or she see themselves and you playing?

7.   If your family were everything you wanted it to be, how
       would you describe it in a word or a phrase?
       How would he or she describe it?

8.   Do you believe in spanking or mild corporal punishment as
       part of disciplining children?
       Does your prospective mate?

Comments

       These questions are open ended because there are as many
answers as there are people, and while some answers are better than
others, many will work as long as there is basic agreement between

the two of you. What you need to look for are the areas of agreement and disagreement and to decide how well you can work together in this most important task of parenting. There may well be things you disagree with so strongly that you should not get married. If one of you wants children and the other really does not, don't marry. This is not something you can agree to disagree about. If you are both uncertain at this point, you need to at least decide that if one of you really does want to have children later, the other can live with the decision.

Question 1 and 2. Besides just saying that you want to have children, this is a good chance to talk about why. If you read the popular magazines, every star in Hollywood wants to have children with or without the benefit of marriage or even without a partner in raising them. Often I get the impression it is merely to prove a point (Michael Jackson, Madonna?) or because it is a status symbol, like another toy or award. Of course, most of these same people can afford nannies and can pack the children off to private schools so they do not interfere with their careers. The sad story of the majority of Hollywood children is that they don't turn out very well. Egotistical celebrities don't make very good parents.

But what about you? Why do you want to have children? Are they an extension of you or someone you need to love you? Are they someone on whom you are willing to lavish love and attention, or are they all right as long as they don't get in the way of your career and other plans? These are important questions. As someone once said, "Any two fools can make a baby. Raising a decent human being takes wisdom and smart teamwork."

Don't skip over these questions, and look critically at the differences in your answers if there are some. Are they differences that spell selfishness or lack of preparedness to do the hard work that raising a child requires? If so, beware. Being the only parent in a marriage is not the way God intended it to work.

Question 3. The number of children you want to have is something you should be in basic agreement about ahead of time.

It may be something you reconsider later. My brother's wife thought she wanted six until after the second one! Both were happy to compromise at that point. If you want two or three and your partner wants only one, are you willing to compromise? Will you feel put upon if you do?

Question 4. Again, look for areas of agreement or disagreement. Does your intended want to wait until you have a house and some money in the bank so that one of you can stay home and raise children full time, while you want to start a family right away? If so, you may have a big problem. The story of wives who reluctantly agree to wait but then "forget" to take the birth control pills is a common one. The result is often a very rocky marriage. Resentment and economic hardship put a lot of strain on what should be a happy time. (If this is a pattern in your prospective mate's family, watch out! It will tend to repeat itself.)

Question 5. Raising children does require sacrifice. There are sacrifices of time, privacy, and sleep, of doing just what you want to do, of energy, of attention, of freedom. There are sometimes sacrifices of career plans, financial goals, and sacrifices that cause emotional and physical pain, especially if a child is seriously ill or handicapped. Are you or your prospective mate aware of at least some of the sacrifices? Are you together willing and able to put children ahead of your own needs, should that be necessary? Will your intended be a supporter or a whiner?

Question 6. Before you marry is a good time for this assessment. If one of you says, "I'll be willing to have children, but raising them is going to be your job," how well does that fit your expectations? If one of you wants to do anything but change diapers, can you live with that? If one of you is uncomfortable about disciplining the kids and wants you to do it all, will that work for you? Some of these things are obviously more important than others, but parenting works best when it is done together and when the two of you agree on how you will handle challenges as they come along. If one person ends up as the disciplinarian while the other is always the good guy, your child will quickly learn to manipulate you. This is the worst lesson they can learn. Having a parent who is remote or detached is almost as bad as having none at all. So look at these areas of agreement and disagreement carefully.

Question 7. What do these answers tell you? Is there enough similarity in your vision of the family to make it work together. Don't settle for a simplistic, one-word answer like "happy." Why is it happy? What would you have to do to produce a family that operates as you envision it? This is a great question for a long discussion. Pay attention to what he or she is saying. Don't let her or him get by with passively agreeing with you. What do they really feel?

You may get some important family history at this point; for instance, if he or she says, "I want it to be a peaceful family, not where dad and mom are fighting all the time or throwing things." Remember, children often repeat family patterns, even unwillingly. If your intended grew up in a home where fighting or abuse was the norm, he or she may need counseling to overcome the legacy of that past. Now is the time to get it before he or she brings that baggage into your marriage.

Question 8. Whether or not you believe in spanking or corporal punishment is not as important as that you both agree. If you disagree, one of you will end up interfering with discipline, rescuing the child, or causing a great deal of resentment on the part of the other and undermining them to the point that proper discipline will be impossible. It is very important to agree here. Nothing can cause more havoc or result in more heartache than parents who don't agree and fail to present a united front to their children.

If you both agree that you do not want to use corporal punishment, you do need to figure out what forms of rewards and punishment you will use. Children do need discipline, and they learn good behavior by being rewarded for it, and being punished when they misbehave. Time out, sitting in a corner, missing a favorite activity, and a host of other options are available. They should be used even if you spank.

A word of caution: While I do not feel that spanking is inappropriate, it is not the same as using a belt, a wooden paddle, or anything else that will cause bruising or welts, or any injury to a child. If your prospective mate was treated with and believes in using such force, think long and hard about this relationship. It may be that he or she was the victim of abuse, and may well be capable of repeating that pattern with your children. This calls for some more questions, and probably for some counseling to deal with the cause of this thinking.

On a positive note, the senior class of our local high school was asked to nominate people who they thought were the best parents in town. They recognized five sets of parents at their graduation as the people they thought had done a great job of raising their children and were people they would go to if they needed to talk or had a problem. Interestingly, they were the same people I would have chosen had I been asked. They all had some very important things in common.

They were all people of faith—one couple was Catholic, one Baptist, and three were Presbyterians—and all active in their churches. They all had been advisers or helpers for the youth groups of their churches. They liked kids and liked to be around their kids' friends. They worked to make sure there were healthy things for their children and friends to do. And they provided a listening ear for kids who had trouble at home or school, and encouraged them to do their best.

The fathers were all involved in their children's activities. For some, that involved considerable effort, as they drove logging and lumber trucks, leaving sometimes at 3:00 A.M. and returning at 6:00 P.M. They still managed to get to games, concerts, and support their kids at weekend activities. Their families were a top priority.

They were very much together on discipline. You could tell their children knew the security of not being able to play one parent off against the other. They knew that even if Dad were gone a lot, he would care enough to back Mom up. I learned a lot of parenting skills by watching some of these families operate. I noticed that they communicated with each other, knew what each other's kids were doing, and learned from each other.

Not surprisingly, their children turned out well. Some are outstanding successes; others are just really solid citizens who are raising their kids the way they saw Mom and Dad do it. Our world is a better place because these parents cared. And not just their own children benefited—other kids got to see a positive model as well. As you consider whom to marry, remember that the right choice affects not only you, but future generations as well.

We've dealt with the big three causes of marital problems, but there are a few more areas to consider. Press on...the right person for you does exist!

Chapter 7

Some Previous Attachments

Happy families are all alike; every unhappy family is unhappy in its own way.

Leo Tolstoy in Anna Karenina

Up to this point, most of the questions have assumed that your prospective mate was single and had no children. If that is true of you and him or her, you can skip this chapter. We encounter a different set of challenges when that is not the case, and there are definite issues you need to face if you are contemplating marrying someone who is divorced or widowed and has children.

If you are involved with someone who is already married to someone else, the best advice is to stop right now. The likelihood of that person divorcing their spouse and marrying you is quite low, no matter what they tell you. Statistically, nearly ninety percent of married men having an affair do not marry the "other woman." And the probability of having a happy marriage with them if they do is also quite low. After all, if they are willing to cheat on their spouse now, what makes you think they won't do that to you after the novelty wears off? Read Dear Abby, Ann Landers, Meg, or any advice column—they are filled with the stories of people unhappily caught in that trap.

Better yet, consider the case of Krystal and Leon. Leon was married, had a six-year-old son, and another child on the way when he met Krystal, a co-worker from another department in the company where he worked. He had been married seven years to a woman he had met in college. They had married because they "had to," but they both finished college and he had done his internship and had become established in his business. He was not particularly ambitious, but steady; a non-drinker, seemingly reliable, seemingly happy.

Krystal was married, too, and had a six-year-old son. But she was bored. Her husband was a steady, good man who wasn't much for excitement or parties. The men at work seemed a lot more interesting, and she especially liked Leon. He had a more prestigious job and more money (she thought). She set out to get him, and very quickly their relationship grew into an affair, complete with partying and drinking. It might have stayed there, except that her husband got wind of it and started divorce proceedings. She started pressuring Leon to tell his wife and when she found out without him telling her first, they separated. Messy divorces followed. Both parental families got involved. His family practically disowned him for his immoral behavior and sided with his wife. Her family did much the same. Almost in defiance, they got married and soon had a child.

Over the years, Leon's former wife moved far away and remarried. He lost contact with the children after a couple of visitations and fell behind in support payments. Krystal hadn't liked having them there for visits anyhow and resented the money going out to children that weren't hers. Leon finally got so far behind that he accepted the new husband's offer to adopt them. The break was pretty much complete. He patched up things with his folks, but Krystal was never really made to feel very welcome in his family, as they kept plenty of reminders of their contact with his children around.

After a few more years, Krystal's need for something more resurfaced. An affair with an employee in her new company led to her moving in with a new lover. Leon and Krystal divorced. He kept her boy and their daughter with him most of the time, but not much else from their marriage. She remarried someone new she met after the live-in arrangement blew up, and life went on for her. Life went on for Leon, too, but he was shorn of his children from his first marriage and a great deal of money, and filled with regrets for lost and damaged relationships. The story is sad, true, and rather typical. Don't let it be yours.

If you are thinking about marrying someone who is widowed or divorced, or if you are widowed or divorced yourself, you do need to deal with some realities that you can't afford to ignore if the two or more of you are going to be a happy family. Sometimes "love's more comfortable the second time around," but it takes someone who is mature and able to handle the complexities of life with ex-family members involved to make it work. Here are some questions to consider: *(Circle answers that apply)*

1. What is your marital status?
    Single, never married   Widowed   Divorced
    Divorced more than once
    Single, ended long-term relationship

    If formerly married, how long has it been since you ended that marriage or relationship? _____ Did you get counseling before or after the breakup? _____

2. What is your prospective mate's marital status?
    Single, never married   Widowed   Divorced
    Divorced more than once
    Single, ended long-term relationship

    If formerly married, how long has it been since she or he ended that marriage or relationship? _____ Did they get counseling before or after the breakup? _____

3.   Are there still a lot of hard feelings and difficulties left over
     from the former relationship?
     For You: Yes, on my part   No, on my part
     Yes, on ex's part   No, on ex's part
     For Mate: Yes, on their part   No, on their part
     Yes, on ex's part   No, on ex's part
     How difficult do you think these will be to deal with?

4.   Are there children? No *(Skip to comments or go to
     questions for Chapter 8)*
     Yes; mine, ages _____
     Yes; his or hers, ages _____

5.   Who has custody? Yours: _____   Prospective mate's ____
     Have visitation rights, times, and places been clearly estab-
     lished?   Yes   No   Joint custody
     Are you comfortable with the arrangements?   Yes   No
     Don't know

6.   Have you met your prospective mate's children?   Yes   No
     If yes, do you like them?   Yes   No
     Do they like you?   Yes   No

     Has he or she met your children?   Yes   No
     If yes, does he or she like them?   Yes   No
     Do they like him or her?   Yes   No

7.   If there are grandparents on either side, have you and your
     prospective mate met them?   Yes   No
     Are they willing to accept you and him or her as part of the
     family?   Yes   No

Comments

     The relationships involved in marriages between people who
have had previous marriages and children from those marriages
become immediately more complex than if the two are single and

unmarried. For one thing, there are simply more relationships to manage. But it also can become a bewildering battleground that has sunk many a second marriage if those relationships are not well understood, well worked out, and fairly well healed before you start. Do not underestimate how bad it can get, or how helpless you will feel if things get ugly between a former mate and you and your relatives. Think long and hard about how much you can handle before you leap into this type of relationship.

Question 1 and 2: If either of you is widowed, divorced, or ending a long-term, live-in relationship, the key question is how long has it been since that relationship ended? Every reputable counselor I know recommends that people wait at least a year before getting back into another committed relationship. It takes that long to heal from the hurt, anger, betrayal, and loss that accompanies a break up. Unfortunately, many people do not wait, and sometimes even begin a new relationship during or before the old one ends. This is one reason why so many second marriages do not work out (the failure rate is worse than fifty percent). Please don't make that mistake.

Give yourselves the time it takes to heal those old hurts and stabilize the feelings and relationships involved. Especially if there are children involved, take your time. They need to come to terms with the loss and pain, too, before they can go on to a new relationship. To expect them or you to process all the anger, grief, and change in any less time is simply unrealistic. If you arrest the process by moving too quickly, the process will stop, and the rage and pain will come out later in worse ways than if it had been dealt with earlier.

Children and adults will often have difficulty making a healthy attachment to the new person in their lives if they haven't detached or come to terms with the ending of the old relationship. It is especially complicated if the child has to relate to a new mother or father when the old one is still around. And that is true even if the parents don't use the child in a tug of war against each other.

A lot of wisdom and patience is required if you are the new person in the relationship. You will be tempted to compare yourself to the former spouse, win the children away from that loyalty, and take their place. You will be disappointed if you find that is not possible. The children may play on those feelings to get away with things they would not get away with at home. If this sounds discouraging, it sometimes really is.

You will need to read up on how to be a stepparent, and you may need to get some professional help going in. It is a big challenge. There are divorce recovery groups and family therapists who specialize in helping blended families. Give yourself some time to figure out how you will handle all this. Now is a good time to really talk it through with your prospective mate. He or she needs to be clear on what they expect and how they will help you navigate these challenges.

Question 3. Don't minimize the difficulties if there is still real friction between you and your ex, or your prospective mate and his or her ex. It is natural for the ex-spouse to resent you, even if they have remarried. They will not be happy having their children in your care, even for visits. If you have never been married and are entering a situation in which there is an ex-spouse and children, don't underestimate the amount of trouble this can cause. This is especially true if the ex regards you as the person who broke up their marriage (whether that is true or not), or if they see you as a possible threat in a future battle for custody of the children.

First, you need to know where things stand. Does your prospective mate, or you, need more time to work things out and calm relations with the ex(s) involved? By all means take it before getting married. Are there still court hearings pending on custody, child support, etc? You should ask to see the decree and the relevant proceedings. Don't be like the women who find out five years later that the divorce was never finalized! The point is that you need to know what you are getting into.

It would be best if all the issues that can be resolved are resolved before you get married. Will all of your mate's income be tied up settling the previous marriage, with you ending up supporting both of you? Will the ex make your life miserable with constant court battles? Has your prospective spouse settled things as fairly and honorably as possible with their former mate? (If he or she hasn't, what makes you think they will treat you honorably in the new marriage?) Have you settled things fairly and honorably, if you are formerly married? If there are major problems, you will be better off ending the relationship now than getting into a bigger mess down the line. Divorces do not get easier the second time around!

Question 4, 5, and 6. If there are children, either from your former marriage or your prospective mate's, be aware that not all blended families get along as well as the Brady Bunch. The Bradys didn't seem to have any ex-spouses or grandparents around, and they had that wonderful mediator, Alice, to cook, clean, and mend their relationships. There are real adjustments to be made, and not all children or adults make them easily.

As the adults involved, you do have a right to a happy relationship without a veto by your children, but realistically, you need to look carefully before committing yourself and your children to a relationship that makes someone really unhappy. If he or she has children, do you really like them? This is crucial if your intended has custody and you will be the one who is around the children the most. Are they spoiled brats, or children who are comfortable to be around? Will he or she expect you to take an active part in raising them, and back you up in disciplining them, or not? All of these are very important issues if you are to have a happy home.

In general, the younger the children are, the more easily they will make the adjustment of accepting a new parent in their lives. With older children, you may have to really work out carefully how they want to be treated, what they want to call you, and what the rules will be in the new situation. You will most probably never be their "real" mom or dad, and the choice of how to relate to them has to be a mutual decision. And if there are ex-spouses in the picture, and they decide to use the children in an emotional tug of war, you need to be prepared for a lot of debriefing and emotional unloading when children come back from visits. You will need a lot of wisdom and support from your spouse to stay out of the middle of the battle and to pick up the pieces.

Just how badly do you want to do all this? If you really aren't sure you like his or her children, or if they don't seem to like you, or if you both have children who don't seem to get along well, or your children don't like your prospective mate (children are sometimes good judges of character), you are most probably not going to have a happy marriage.

Custody issues that may arise depend a lot on what the circumstances of the divorce were, and on the courts. Courts and judges absolutely hate to get in the middle of custody fights, and prefer to award joint custody these days and let the parents battle it out. That is not always a great solution, as the spouses have a million ways of changing visiting times and evading responsibilities, if they wish. If there are set rules, it can help you know what to expect. If not, what is your best estimate of how that ex-spouse is going to be about making visitation a pleasant or unpleasant experience? How does your intended mate feel about visitation? Is he or she going to be a basket case every time the kids come or go?

Incidentally, courts tend to regard visitation and child support as two separate issues. Just because the parent is not sending support doesn't mean the other parent can deny visitation. However, courts are getting better about enforcing support, and sometimes a parent who is reluctant to pay support or gets way behind might consent to adoption instead, so that he (usually) can get out of the burden. Sometimes non-custodial parents will lose interest over time and make life less difficult for the children and the new family. But don't count on it. Kids themselves have some say in whether they will visit or which parent they stay with after the age of fourteen (in some states, such as Texas, judges will listen to kids of ten or twelve). You may have to endure for a long time the disruption that visitation causes. Do you want to?

Blended families can and do work. But there are a lot of things to consider. Look before you leap, and talk about the possible scenarios with your intended mate ahead of time. Don't minimize the difficulties, and plan ahead. Much depends on how willing the two of you are to work together and be sensitive to all the emotions that are in play. It is not easy, but if this is the right person for you and the right mix for the children, you can make a happy family.

Question 7. This final question about grandparents is more important than you might think. Like it or not, the children have grandparents on the ex-spouse's side, and they have feelings, relationships, and, in some states, even rights. They will most probably want to keep up the relationship with their grandchildren, whether they like you or not, or like your intended spouse or not. It will be a whole lot easier if the relationship is good. In one sense, grandparents are the unintended victims of a divorce. They tend to lose out through no fault of their own. They will tend to side with their child out of loyalty, but sometimes they will side with the spouse if there was infidelity, drugs, or alcohol involved. No matter what, there will always be discomfort in the relationship, and when the spouse remarries they have to do a lot of adjusting to be able to welcome someone new raising their grandchild. Some do it graciously and willingly; some can be the grandparents from hell.

Have you met them? Do you have a sense of what they will be like? How will they treat your children? These are good questions to ponder now. These are good things to talk about with your prospective mate now. Will he or she manage that relationship or will they expect you to do so? How will you split time at holidays, vacations, etc. to keep everyone happy? There are a lot of things to manage, and the more you talk about it now, the better off you will be. If it looks like a really messy situation in which a lot of hard feelings and disruptive behavior are involved, be aware that relatives can cause an amazing amount of grief. If you need to have some time to heal the relationships or work out amicable solutions, by all means do so before you marry. It will save much misery later on.

One final thought: a person who goes through the rejection of a divorce will often need a lot of assurance about their own worth, their ability to keep a new mate's love, their sex appeal, and much more. No mate can supply all of that, no matter how hard you try. They will tend to find it harder to trust a new mate, particularly if there was infidelity involved. They may be more realistic about marriage and what they want, and they may be more mature from having gone through the experience, if they have had time to heal. But if, understandably, they are left embittered, still very entangled in battles left from the divorce, and angry, they are probably not ready to get married again. Don't rush in. They need to have time, *at least a year or more;* and they probably need professional help before you should think of marrying.

The story of Leon and Krystal has a flip side to it. Leon's wife, in the aftermath of the divorce, found a strong new faith and resolved not to let life get her down. She dealt with the grief and betrayal, went back to school, and got an advanced degree. She found a great job in a city far away and started anew. She took her children to church, where she eventually met a man who really loved her and her children, and supported her through some trying times with the ex-spouse. Her children loved Mark and accepted him as their new father. They accepted a new baby sister, too. They grew up to be very normal and successful people and love being a close family to this day.

It can happen that way. But it takes a lot of planning, praying, and hard work to make it happen. Take a good hard look at what you face if you're planning to marry someone with a family. It may be hard, but if you're sure he or she is the right one, you've worked out the issues together carefully, and you're both willing to work hard to make it work, go for it with God's help.

So much for this rather complicated subject. There are just a few more questions on the road to finding that person who is just right for you.

Chapter 8

Violence

Pansies! Rosemary! Violence! My wedding bouquet!
Edward Albee, *Who's Afraid of Virginia Woolf?*

One of the world's unhappiest nightmares is to wake up one day and find you are married to a violently abusive person. While this was thought to be pretty much of a male thing, more light has shown that women, too, are capable of being abusers. And we are beginning to realize that it is a much bigger problem than we had thought. People die every day from being beaten, thrown down stairs, being smashed against walls, etc. Children as well as spouses suffer, and the horrifying thing is that there is probably much more abuse that goes unreported and undetected. There is a syndrome that occurs when one person dominates another that causes the abused person to become so terrified that they lose their ability to resist or escape. Once the pattern gets established, abused spouses leave only to end up going back again and again, and sometimes they are killed.

So this chapter is really a matter of life and death. One question is how can we avoid becoming the victim of someone who is going to be violent and abusive? I'm going to suggest as a starting point two attitudes that you need to have before going into any serious relationship. One is simply that *you do not deserve to be beaten or hit by anyone who says they love you.* If you think you are such a bad person that someone ought to punish you, or that beating and punishment are part of love, then I suggest that you get help immediately. Talk to your minister, priest, rabbi, or any reputable counselor. You are a perfect setup for an abusive person, and you need help before you are caught in a cycle of violence. Beating is not any part of a healthy and loving relationship. While some people seem to enjoy sadomasochistic sex games, and so-called rough sex, it is a short step from there into violence and abuse. If your prospective mate is "into" this, beware. This behavior tends to make you an object rather than a person. That alone should make you uncomfortable.

The second attitude is what I call *"One strike and you're out!"* I believe that you need to announce early in the relationship that you don't believe violence has any place in a loving relation-ship, and that if he or she ever hits you, you are gone. You have to mean it when you say it, but this kind of prevention is the best defense you have against being trapped in a cycle of violence. The pattern of the abuser is always to be very penitent, say that they did not mean to hurt you, that somehow something you said or did pushed them over the edge, and that it will never happen again. Do not believe them! They think they mean what they say but they don't, except for the part about it being your fault that they acted the way they did. That is the classic reasoning of the abuser. This attitude will protect you and it will tell your prospective mate where the boundaries are. Sometimes it is enough to curb any violent tendencies that a normal person might have, too. If a mate knows that they can never hit you, it prevents arguments from escalating into violence and bloodshed.

You should probably make the same "One strike and you're out" statement about your children, too. Whether you have any at this point or not, now is a good time to build a wall around their happiness also. At the very least, it will give you a chance to discuss child raising and the kind of discipline that is and is not appropriate. You may uncover some key information about how he or she was raised that will give you clues about their future behavior.

But the violent person is not always easy to spot. Take the case of Jim and Jenny. When I first met them, they seemed like the cutest, shyest, most mild-mannered couple I had ever seen. They had an adorable baby girl, about three months old, who had their same blonde good looks, and who looked as if she were really loved and cared for. I learned that they were both scientists, she a biochemist and he a physical chemist doing research for a large company.

He came to see me first. He said they were having some disagreements over how to handle their new parenthood, and he was concerned that Jenny seemed almost too protective and withdrawn since the baby's birth. The information he volunteered seemed rather vague, and he talked very precisely and tersely, which I thought that perhaps a person who spent a lot of time in a laboratory might do. I suggested that I could help better if I could talk to both of them together and we set an appointment.

When we got together, the time available was short and they brought the baby, who was very distracting. Jenny didn't say much, and seemed almost as unemotional as Jim had been. I made appointments to see them separately, as I had the feeling he was pushing me to get her to do or say more but she wasn't going to in his presence. But the appointment got moved to her house, and between a neighbor's phone call and a doctor's appointment for the baby being moved up, the time was shortened and nothing was accomplished except that she seemed to be a little more comfortable talking to me. She apologized over and over for how messy the house was, though it wasn't. Something didn't seem right, but I wasn't sure what.

I saw Jim again and had the similar sensation that I was missing something. He complained that their sex life was nonexistent since the baby had arrived, and that she wouldn't go anywhere without her. I explained that this was not unusual for a first time mother with a baby that age. We went on to how they communicated and I asked him if he always spoke in such an unemotional tone, and he said that if he didn't they couldn't communicate. He kept insisting that she needed to talk more, and I felt again that he was hoping I could make her change. As he left, he mentioned that things were not going well at work, but it was in such an unemotional and "in passing" way that I didn't really ask about it.

I tried to set a time to see Jenny, but kept missing her. Finally, one morning, I caught her on the phone. She was obviously upset. At first she told me only that Jim had quit his job, and that she didn't know what they were going to do. I heard noises in the background and she finally admitted that a neighbor was there, and I heard someone say, "Is that the police?" Sobbing, she let the story out. Jim had begun acting so strangely at work that he had been fired. He had come home in a rage and had hit her when she tried to calm him down. It hadn't been the first time. The neighbor was urging her to call the police and get protection. She wanted to get in touch with her mother in Atlanta and get away. I suggested she do both, and gave her the number of a lawyer who could help.

Jenny did get away, and Jim was forced to get therapy. I don't know whether they ever got back together, since they both moved away, but I learned a valuable lesson. You can't tell an abuser just by looking at them. Jim was the last person you would ever have expected to be capable of beating anyone. But underneath that calm, seemingly concerned and loving demeanor was a boiling rage that spilled over violently into their marriage. I had the impression that they were so shy that they had drifted into marriage without knowing much about each other except that they both had a love of scientific investigation in common. Unfortunately, they didn't do enough investigation of each other before marrying.

Abused women, in research done over the past few years, have pointed out one sign of the abuser, which is that they are often overly affectionate, considerate, polite, or romantic at first. They really know how to "hook" you. They will overwhelm you with love notes, flowers, and gifts. You will think that they are just too good to be true. As with business scams that sound too good to be true, they *are* too good to be true. They will often seem so mild mannered that you will not suspect them of the violence that they are concealing.

Rather soon, the relationship will become confining. He or she will attempt to monopolize your time, control who you see, tell you how to dress, and limit the time you spend with parents or family. He or she may do so very subtly—it will always supposedly be for your good—but you will gradually become isolated from anyone but them. If you feel yourself becoming confined or smothered in a relationship, beware. Step back, do some investigation, and be prepared to get out fast if it looks like you may be in the hands of a potentially violent person.

Here are some questions that you can use to identify the potentially violent person. These questions are not foolproof, and they need to be supplemented with plenty of observation and feedback from others who might know your prospective mate better. As always, what the person *does* is more important than what they *say.* *(Circle answers)*

1. Does your prospective mate have a "hot temper?"
    Yes   No

2. Does he/she seem angry a lot of the time they are around you?   Yes   No

3. Has your prospective mate ever hit you?   Yes   No
    Intentionally?   Yes   No

4. Has he or she hit anyone of opposite sex?   Yes   No
    Intentionally?   Yes   No

5. Does he or she handle anger by throwing things?
    Yes   No
    Hitting things?   Yes   No
    Smashing things?   Yes   No

6.   How does his or her family handle anger? Specifically, is there any pattern of violence between his or her parents? Yes   No
     Between other family members?   Yes   No

7.   Is there any history of abuse in his or her family?
     Yes   No
     Was he or she abused physically or sexually?   Yes   No

8.   Has he or she ever abused a cat, dog, or other pet?
     Yes   No

9.   Does he or she have a criminal record for violent behavior?
     Yes   No

Comments

The questions above seem simple enough, but it is amazing how often they do not get asked. If, as Shakespeare said, "Love is blind, and lovers cannot see the petty follies that themselves commit," this is the point at which you need to open your eyes and not ignore any signs that you see. Too much is at stake. Violence is not petty. You may have to dig a bit to get the answers to some of these questions. You may not be able to ask them directly. If the person seems unusually angry about something that a family member has said, it might be a good time to ask them why that person really seems to get to them. You may get a lot of family history at that point. Listen to it carefully. Is there anything that would lead you to suspect a violent side to the relationships?

Often people can't or won't talk about abuse or family violence. They may have buried it deeply, been threatened not to reveal family secrets, or not be able to consciously recall it without therapy. So look for signs. Is there someone in the family who seems very controlling, and to whom everyone else defers? Is there someone who appears very dominated, repressed, or fearful? Is the family open, or do there seem to be secrets that no one can tell? If the answer to some of these questions is yes, suspect abuse or violence and dig deeper. Abusive patterns tend to repeat themselves from generation to generation.

Questions 1 and 2. These are early but very clear warning signals of a violence prone individual. "Hot tempered" is usually a euphemism used to excuse a violent temper. If other people describe your prospective mate in this way, take heed. You may use the words "misunderstood" or say that "people always seem to pick on him (or her) and he (or she) gets into fights." If you do, be aware that you are *already* excusing and enabling his or her conduct! And that is a bad sign. He or she has hooked you emotionally into feeling sorry for them and into condoning their behavior.

But while he or she may not be directing their anger or violence at you now, they will tend to abuse their rescuers later on. If your prospective mate seems to be angry a lot of the time, remember that their anger will have to be expressed somewhere. If they are getting into fights, causing unpleasant scenes with sales or service people, being kicked out of bars or restaurants, or jumping into arguments in which they aren't directly involved, you are looking at an angry and potentially violent and abusive person. This is not the mate for you.

Question 3. If your prospective mate has ever hit you intentionally, go back in your mind over what happened. Was there an abject apology? Did you end up taking the blame somehow for making him or her so angry? If so, you are dealing with the classic pattern of abusive reasoning. You need to get out of this relationship *right now* before you begin believing that somehow you are responsible for *their* violence. You may have to deal with tears, threats, and whining, but that is preferable to anything down the road. If he or she is willing to get long-term help for their problem, and you are willing to wait for them, fine. But do it at a distance and do not date or see each other until treatment is completed, and don't accept any half measures or statements of good intentions. Some people never really are able to admit they are violent and get real help. (O.J. Simpson is a case in point.)

If your prospective mate has hit you more than once, or you are in a relationship in which you are being repeatedly abused either verbally or physically, call the nearest abuse hotline, women's or men's, and get out of the situation. Do it for you, for your children, for your mother, or for me, but **get out now!** Your life is in danger. (See Chapter 13.)

Question 4. If your prospective mate has never hit you, but has hit others of the opposite sex, this is a serious sign. It is astonishing to me that many women said they would date O.J. Simpson even after hearing the 911 tapes of Nicole calling for help and screaming as she was being battered by him. Sometimes people are abusive only to the one person who knows how to "push their buttons," but most often an abuser is an abuser.

If your prospective mate has hit others, has he or she gotten help? Is their explanation of it different from that of the person that got hit? (You really ought to talk to that person if possible.) Don't assume the violence will not be repeated. Declare your "one strike and you're out" policy, and think long and hard about where this is going. If this was a serious or repeated incident and they don't admit their problem and don't get help, you should not continue this relationship.

Question 5. Throwing, hitting, or smashing things is not as serious as hitting or smashing you, but it does indicate a lot of anger, and a certain amount of emotional immaturity. (If the things he or she throws come flying at you, that's also quite dangerous.) You might want to ask them why they throw things or smash things. Is that the way his or her family did things? Family patterns do tend to repeat themselves, and this may reveal a pattern of violence in their family.

It becomes a pretty expensive habit, too. Do you always want to be replacing dishes and furniture? Now is the time to seek help in dealing with the anger and lack of self-control. It will be much harder to deal with later on. It is not really a large step from smashing things to smashing you.

Question 6. Getting the family history is important, as is observing their family closely. In some families, emotions are worn on the sleeve. They may be noisy, excitable, even argumentative, but you can sense the love and respect. The more closed, secretive, and unemotional family may seem to be the calmer family, but may be hiding deeper problems. A few families may openly show themselves to be violent, but most hide it.

If you have a feeling that deeper emotions lie beneath the surface, particularly anger or hostility, do some checking, and try to get your prospective mate to talk about it. Rest assured, this person will probably say something like, "Dad hit me a lot, but I mostly deserved it," or, "I didn't get it nearly as bad as Mom or my sister." These are really statements of denial. They do *not* mean that the emotional scars have healed or that the person will not become abusive toward you. In fact, abusive people are almost always people who were abused themselves. You may want to ask people who know the family what they think.

Question 7. This may be the hardest question about which to get a direct answer. But if you get an indication that your prospective spouse has been the victim of physical or sexual abuse, be aware that most child abusers were abused themselves, and that close to ninety percent of violent criminals were physically abused themselves. It is a repeating pattern that is tragic if it is not interrupted. If your prospective mate was abused and did not get long-term help, they need to do so now before you go any further. (See comments in Chapter 5, Question 5) Both sexual and physical abuse cause emotional damage that you cannot undo. The person needs professional help, and the only constructive thing you can do is point them toward it and get out of the way while they get it.

Question 8. If you overhear your prospective mate talking about drowning cats, setting their tails on fire, or torturing animals as if they enjoyed it, be aware that this is often a sign of very disturbed and violent behavior. If they show remorse now, as if it were some sort of a childish prank that they did before they knew better, do a little digging for the whole story, which may in the end qualify as more normal. But if they seem to be cruel to animals (and I am not talking about hunting), you won't enjoy being around them much, and it may be a sign that you could be in for the same kind of treatment. Do not dismiss your feelings about any sort of quirky behavior. Ask yourself if you will want to live with that day in and day out. For your sake, I hope the answer is no. Point your friend to a therapist and see whether they go there.

Question 9. This question is worth asking if you have even a hint that the person is violent. Police will tell you whether a person has a record of arrests and or convictions for violent behavior, or at least will tell you if a person has a clean record. All they need from you to look it up is a date of birth and a social security number. A detective can get the information, if you can't. If the person does have a record, find out what it is for. If violence is involved, this is very good grounds for deciding that this is not the person you want to marry.

One of the unhappiest young women I've ever met is a beautiful girl who drifts from one unsatisfying relationship to the next. She looks as though she could have her choice of any young man she wants, but she keeps on choosing real losers who exploit her, get her to take care of their kids or responsibilities, and then dump her. She has acquired a really loose reputation, mostly deserved, and she can't seem to make good decisions about men. If you delved into her past, there are good reasons for her lack of self-esteem and poor judgment. But the saddest statement she made to someone who was asking her why she didn't get away from the current boyfriend who was clearly using her, was, "Well, at least he doesn't beat me up much."

She needs therapy. She is a heartbeat away from final self-destruction, but she is not atypical of the candidates for marriage who are perfect setups for an abusive relationship. You don't have to be as messed up as she is to also fall for the line of a violent person. I hope you use this chapter wisely and look your intended over very carefully. It really is a matter of life and death. If you need to get out, see Chapter 13.

On to the next subject. There are plenty of good people who don't have violent pasts and futures out there, so don't give up hope or settle for a nightmare. You deserve better!

Chapter 9

In-Laws or Outlaws?

One would be in less danger from the wiles of the stranger
If ones own kin and kith were more fun to be with.

Ogden Nash, Family Court

Jill was getting edgy. It was always that way when Bob's parents were about to arrive for their annual visit—"Inspection tour" was what she really called it when they couldn't hear. It seemed like nothing she ever did was quite right or good enough for her mother-in-law. There were always the veiled put-downs; and the implication that she and Bob were raising their family "strangely different from the way they had done things" grated on their nerves. Bob's father was always telling him how he should be fixing the house or running his finances, which was at least helpful, but seemed to make Bob look and feel helpless.

The kids were subjected to a constant stream of unasked for advice on how they should act when they went out, how they should dress, and what they should eat. By the time the visit was over, they practically had to be forced to see them off at the airport. It had taken a couple of weeks to debrief and decompress the emotions left from the last visit. They all agreed that it was a good thing that they lived a long way away, because once a year was about all they could stand. As Jill dusted and vacuumed every inch of the house, she wondered how they would survive this round. She also wondered how Bob could have turned out so differently from his family.

Many a marriage has suffered through a constant war of nerves and words centered around parents, and parents-in-law; some have actually been torn apart by the struggle. For better or worse, when you marry someone, their parents come along as part of the package, as do yours. You need to look them over pretty well and make the best decisions you can, based on your estimation of how everyone involved will get along. Often, such choices as where you live, vacation, and work are decided by these relation-ships. So this is a good time for talking about and preparing for the road ahead. Here are some questions that will help you evaluate these important relationships: *(Circle answers where applicable)*

1.   Have you met your prospective mate's parents?   Yes   No
      (If No, and it is not possible to meet them before you marry, you should talk to your mate about them and attempt to answer as many of the rest of these questions as you can, based on the information he or she supplies.)

2.   Do you like them?   Yes   No   Not sure
      Do they make you feel welcome?   Yes   No   Not sure
      Do you feel comfortable around them?
      Yes   No   Not sure
      If No, why not? _____

3.   Do they like you?   Yes   No   Not sure
      How do they feel about you as a prospective mate for their son or daughter? _____
      _____

4.   How possessive are they about their son or daughter? Do they want him or her to be independent, or to be around *them* all of the time? Will they feel his or her first loyalty is to you or them? Do they control his or her job or fortune?

5.   Has your prospective mate met your parents?   Yes   No (If No, and it is not possible for them to meet before you marry, answer the next questions on your best estimate of their reactions. Do not be overly optimistic!)

6.   Does he or she like them?   Yes   No   Not sure
Does he or she feel welcome?   Yes   No   Not sure
Does he or she feel comfortable around them?
Yes   No   Not sure
If No, why not? _____

7.   Do they like him or her?   Yes   No   Not sure
How do they feel about him or her as a prospective mate for their son or daughter? _____
_____

8.   How possessive are they about you? Do they want you to be independent, or to be around *them* all of the time? Will they feel your first loyalty is to you or them? Do they control your job or fortune?

9.   How well do you think your parents will get along with his or her parents?

10.   How close will you be living to your in-laws and your parents? Will there be frequent contact?

11.   Will you be living with either set of parents after you are married?

12.   How important is it to your prospective mate to have good
       relations with your parents and his or hers?
       Very important   Somewhat important   Not important
       Whose responsibility will it be to maintain those relation-
       ships?

Comments

By the fact that I've given you a lot of questions to consider,
you may gather that the whole subject of living with in-laws is a
complex and important one. It is. There are other questions to
consider: Will you have a relative on either side who is really
dysfunctional, alcoholic, or mentally ill, and, if so, how will you
live with that? Is there a family matriarch or patriarch (such as a
grandparent) who controls the family and will be someone you will
have to deal with or avoid? But let's deal with the questions I've
given you first. They should point you to areas you need to discuss
if you haven't already and perhaps avoid some unpleasant surprises
down the road.

Questions 1 and 2. If you have met your prospective in-laws,
take some time to really reflect on how you felt meeting them for the
first time, and how you feel about them now. How do you think they
will be as the grandparents of your children? How do you feel about
them being a part of your life for the next thirty years or so? How
close do you want to be to them? All good questions to ask as you
make your decisions. You do marry the other person's family when
you marry them. You didn't get to choose your own family, but you
can choose whether your intended mate's family is right for you.

Do they know you are a serious prospective mate, or are you
just one of the string of boys or girls that your intended has brought
home? Their attitude may change drastically once they know you
may become a member of the family, so if they aren't clued in take
this into account. Ask your prospective mate if they know how their
parents feel about you or anyone they might marry. If you and your

partner are of different racial or ethnic backgrounds, how will his or her parents react to that? If you and your partner have different religious or social backgrounds, how will they react?

Don't settle for glib answers to any of these questions. "They'll be all right once they get to know you," or "They'll come around eventually (or when their first grandchild comes along)," are not good enough answers. If there are real problems with them accepting you, you need to know if your mate will stick up for you, or if it is going to be necessary to have a long-distance relationship with them. It may not be a reason for not getting married, but it may well determine a lot of decisions you make down the line. It is best to know before you get married, rather than later.

If you have not met your prospective in-laws, and won't be able to before you marry, you can still ask your prospective mate a lot of questions. I'd ask questions like: what their interests are, what they have said about the kind of person they hope he or she will marry, or what their ambitions are for their son or daughter and how will you fit in. Are they fanatic sportsmen, golfers, bridge players? Will they expect you to be a part of that? Will they expect you to spend a lot of time with them, like every Friday for dinner? (These are also good things to discuss even if you have met them!)

You may also want to spend some time with them on the phone. Be sure to share the things you like best about your intended, and listen for their reactions. If you have a feeling that there are things you should tell them about yourself (especially if you have children, or you are of a different race, ethnic group, or religion), tell them in a positive way (for instance, "Maybe Jim has told you that I have two boys. They really love him already, and he is so good with them, etc."). What is their reaction? If it is something like, "Well, Jim always was the one who picked up strays in our family!" you know you've got some problems ahead. If one of them has, or threatens to have, a heart attack, you have really serious problems ahead.

Though this is the family in which your prospective mate grew up, he or she may be very different from them. He or she may have very consciously adopted different values and lifestyles from what their family holds dear. Nonetheless, he or she will see them through the lens of family ties. They are the people that nurtured him or her and there are ties of love there that may allow him or her to shrug off what to you may be outrageous or hurtful comments and actions.

"Oh that's just the way mom is, don't think anything of it," may work for your mate, but will it work for you? Or, "Dad's always teasing, he sounds like a curmudgeon but he's really not mad about anything," may signify an acceptance of behavior you won't want to live with at very close range. If your prospective mate says things like this before you meet them, it might be a good time to probe further. If he or she is not like their parents and is apologizing in advance, why are they so different, and is he or she indicating that the relationship is going to be uncomfortable? If so, will you be living close to them, or does he or she want it to be a distant relationship?

If you have met your prospective in-laws (or if you can sense enough from talking on the phone and from what your prospective mate has told you), how do you feel about them? Do you find it easy to like them? Do they make you feel comfortable and welcome? If you aren't sure, or if the answer is no, stop and analyze why. Is it you or is it them? Are you just very nervous about meeting them, or do you really sense that they don't like you?

This is probably a good time to note that the in-law relationship is nearly always fraught with difficulties. The mother-in-law/daughter-in-law relationship is reportedly the most difficult, because, if you are the daughter-in-law, you are taking away her baby and have become a rival for his affections. There is no one who is good enough to do that in a mother's eyes. On the other hand, there are few fathers who think any young man is really good enough or dependable enough to be caring for his baby girl. In other words, deep down there are some really interesting emotions going on, and you are the outsider.

However, for every in-law from hell, there are also many that are wonderful, caring parents who just want their son or daughter to be happy. The relationship, which can be painful, can also be wonderful if everyone is willing to work at it a little and allow for differences in the way you and your mate will do things. Some of this depends on you. You as the outsider will probably have to meet your in-laws more than half way at first, and do your best to convince them that you want what they want, namely for your intended mate (their child) to be happy and cared for. They in turn should try to make you feel at home in the relationship and not make you feel like you are constantly walking on eggshells or undergoing inspection.

If you felt uncomfortable at first, but things are getting better, that may be normal. If you feel uncomfortable whenever you are around them, and it doesn't seem to get easier, it is time to really look at what is going on. There are plenty of horror stories around that are true and should give you pause. There are the lecherous fathers-in-law that make passes or worse at future daughters-in-law. Your prospective mate needs to be told about this immediately...their reaction will tell you reams about their respect for you, their dependability in defending you, and how the relationship will be in the future—if there's going to be one at all.

There are the imperious and demanding mothers who have their sons securely tied to their apron strings and who will not let go after they are married. Even Franklin D. Roosevelt had such a mother, and she made Eleanor's life a nightmare. Your choices depend on whether he is willing to cut the ties or not, and whether he will be willing to put some distance between her and you. You probably never will be comfortable living close to such an in-law.

There are the "Daddy's girls" who will still put Daddy's ideas, goals, and wishes ahead of yours. If Daddy is wealthy and wants you to join the family business instead of pursuing your own career, she will agree. It may sound comfortable at first, but many an unhappy marriage has been the result. Is Daddy a benevolent tyrant, or a not-so-benevolent one? Are you uncomfortable with the opinions, prejudices, or actions of the family? Are they unethical in some way that disturbs you? These are all good questions to consider carefully at this point, and to talk about tactfully but honestly with your prospective mate.

Question 3. This may sound like the same question, but the fact is that you may like your future in-laws but they may or may not like you. You will probably find the liking or disliking mutual, but they may be good at hiding their feelings. So do they like you, and do they consider you a suitable mate for their child? They may not tell you, so here is where you may have to rely on the honesty of your prospective mate. If he or she won't tell you, or is evasive, you may be able to find out from a friend or relative. But you need to know what they are thinking.

If they regard you as unsuitable because of something they misunderstand, you have a chance to clear it up. If they think you are unsuitable because of something you can and are willing to change, you have a chance to change their opinion. If they think you are unsuitable because they are prejudiced against people of different races, religions, or who are divorced, from the wrong side of the tracks, etc., you may have a chance to change their minds. But you have to know what the problem is, and you have to know whether your prospective mate shares their prejudices. Do they influence him or her to the extent that they will affect your marriage (i.e., is he or she dating or planning on marrying you in order to rebel against their parents?) It is no fun being the lightning rod for an ongoing conflict with your mate's parents!

If your prospective in-laws are extremely prejudiced against you, but your mate knows it, disagrees with them, and will defend you from their behavior, even to the extent of physically distancing the two of you from them, then you have found a gem. But understand that at some point your mate could begin to resent the sacrifice of being away from family, and you might need to make arrangements for them to visit their parents alone, or work out short, infrequent stays, or make some other adjustments. The adjustments will be worthwhile. But you should not be left alone to make the adjustments to in-laws who dislike you. When the chips are down, if your prospective mate is not willing to put your marriage first, ahead of his relationship with his own family, you should not marry.

Please note: I am not talking about imaginary or irrational feelings that your potential in-laws dislike you. Make sure you are dealing with reality. Don't assume that your in-laws won't like you or don't like you. Be yourself around them, treat them as you would want to be treated, and see if they won't respond the same way. Most in-laws will. If you find that they really don't like you or will not accept you no matter what, then you need to decide how you are going to handle that.

Also please note: There are spouses who will demand that you put them ahead of your family, not speak to your family, or who will fight with your family for no particularly good reason, or as proof of your loyalty. They may be almost sickeningly sweet to their face, but then viciously attack them, and you, once your family is gone. If you feel that your potential mate is like this, and that your parents are not at fault, it is a good bet you are dealing with some deeper problem. Your potential mate may come from a family that was dysfunctional, related to each other mainly through conflict, or where they had to deal with alcoholics or abuse. It is a fairly common symptom of codependency that the codependent seems to thrive on causing chaos in family relations. (See comments in Chapter 5.) If that is what you are dealing with, get them to get help or get out of the relationship.

Question 4. Most parents have conflicting feelings about their children. They want them to be on their own and independent, but they also like to feel that they haven't completely lost the relationship they had when their children were younger. It is difficult for parents to treat their children as adults completely, because they remember when they were changing diapers and holding their hands when they crossed the street. But normal parents are not so possessive that they expect the same kind of relationship to extend into adulthood. They don't really want their child to be dependent on them for their livelihood, or to ask their advice on every problem, or to spend all their spare time with them.

Abnormal parents do exist. They cannot let go. They expect their son or daughter to continue to play the same role in the family as they did before they were married, and for the spouse to become absorbed into the family. They expect their child to continue to spend all their spare time with their family and resent any time spent with the spouse's family. Joseph P. Kennedy reportedly kept his sons completely dependent on him for money as a way of making sure they followed his advice. He doled out pocket money to his son John F. Kennedy even after he became President, and played a large part in picking the cabinet of his son's administration. He guided his sons' political careers and paid for their elections. A study of the family reveals a lot of dysfunctional behavior as well as a lot of tragedy.

If a family controls your prospective mate's fortune or livelihood, you can expect that they will have a lot more influence about how he or she spends his time, structures his or her social life, and how you will function in the family as well. If a domestic tyrant heads it, you may find yourself resenting this hold on the two of you very much. Even if the family is a happy one, you still need to ask if you really want to be subject to all of their expectations. You should talk very seriously with your prospective mate about just what those might be.

But a family does not have to be rich or powerful to become a real problem to a potential spouse. In fact, they can be the kind that is so nice that they pull you into their system without your being aware they are doing so. They may not even be aware that they are setting up unreasonable expectations for you. You need to pull back long enough to ask yourself what their expectations are, and what you really want. It may be a tradition for the family to gather for spaghetti dinner on Friday night. But will you be expected to be there every Friday night for the rest of your married life? Do you want to be? Will you be expected to be at their house for every Christmas or will you be able to have your own traditions and share time reasonably with your own family? Now is the time to talk with your potential mate and their family about what the expectations are.

Sometimes, just dealing very directly with potential in-laws is the best. Asking them courteously what their expectations are may be revealing for them and you. They may not have thought through what they do expect, especially if you are their first daughter- or son-in-law. Maybe they don't expect as much as you think, or maybe they will see by talking about things that some expectations aren't reasonable. At any rate, you will find out ahead of time what is really on their minds and whether you can live with that, instead of relying on your vague feelings or worst fears.

Question 5 and 6. Turning the questions around, how does your intended mate like your parents? If they haven't met, how do you think he or she will react to them? If you suspect that he or she might not like them or won't feel comfortable or welcome around them, why is that? Is it because of the way your parents are, or is it something about your prospective mate that you feel will cause problems? If it is something about your parents, is it something you dislike about them, or is it something that you know your prospective mate dislikes?

Do you feel that his or her dislike is reasonable or justified, or is it some kind of bias or prejudice that may be a sign of other personality problems? Remember that you will tend to see your parents in a favorable light and may tend to overlook their faults. But if your potential mate has already taken a dislike to them before he or she has met them, think carefully about whether that dislike is justified. If not, who is at fault? If you have indicated that you are ashamed of your parents or that they have hurt you in some way, you may have aroused your intended's instinct to protect you.

If your intended mate has met your parents, many of the same questions apply. If he or she feels comfortable and welcomed and likes them, you are off to a good start. If not, where does the problem lie? Make sure you understand what he or she is feeling. Is it some kind of insecurity or some misunderstanding of something that was said? Can the perceptions be changed, or are you dealing with something that won't go away? Note that a person's reactions to someone may have nothing to do with the other person. If a person is rich, or successful, or likable, or religious, people may dislike them because they themselves are insecure, envious, or ashamed of what they see as their own shortcomings.

If your mate dislikes your parents because of something they can't help, and you feel that they have treated him or her fairly, you are dealing with emotional problems that will probably get worse after you are married. Do you want to live with that? It will probably mean figuring out how to limit his or her contact with your parents. It will probably mean very uncomfortable times at family gatherings, or no gatherings at all. Think it over carefully. Slow down and get some professional help.

Question 7 and 8. Again, turning the questions around, how do your parents like your intended? If they haven't met, ask yourself honestly how you think they will react. If you are worried about that, is it because of the way *they* are, or is it something about your potential mate that *you* feel they won't like? This may be a good time to ask yourself how well you are communicating with your parents, and how well you understand them. If you are still locked in a battle for independence, and feel they don't understand you, or if they have had a hard time understanding or approving of your choices, you may need to do some work on healing this relationship before springing a potential family member on them.

If you come from a dysfunctional family yourself, are you still enmeshed in their conflicts and games, or have you distanced yourself from them emotionally enough so that you can deal realistically with their reactions to your potential mate? (In other words, if they dislike your prospective mate for some irrational cause, can you keep from taking it personally and deal with whether there is any truth you need to consider, or do you need to dismiss their opinions altogether?)

If your parents have met your intended mate, do you know how they feel about him or her? Sometimes parents won't tell you unless you ask, sometimes they won't say anything at all (maybe by saying nothing they are saying a lot; what is their body language or tone of voice telling you?) Based on previous experience, a smart parent may have figured out that the quickest way to shove you into the arms of someone is to tell you they don't like him or her. And after all, if you are over twenty-one, you are an adult and it is your decision. But if you ask them, telling them that you really want their input but that you know it is not their responsibility to make the decision, they may share their feelings or misgivings.

Listen carefully. You don't need to abide by their feelings, but you do need to understand them. And one thing you know is that they are on your side and they know you and your needs probably better than anyone else does (unless they are alcoholics or otherwise badly dysfunctional). They want what they see as the best for you. They want you to be happy and have a successful marriage.

So if your parents say something like, "Do you know anything about his family?" (implying that they may) or, "You know, she makes me uncomfortable the way she brags a lot and seems to put other people down," or, "Are you sure you want to get involved with a pilot who will be gone so much of the time?" prick up your ears and start listening. They may not be one hundred percent right, but they may be giving you some insights you really need to consider. Most of all, if you can't find some way to ease their misgivings, your mate will have a hard time ever feeling comfortable around them.

Question 9. While it isn't necessary for both sets of parents to get along, it will make life much easier if they do, especially if they both will be living close to you. One of the questions that inevitably comes up is where you will spend holidays and special occasions. While you and your family are still young, it is probably easier for you to go to parents' homes for celebrations, and they will probably want to host such gatherings. To keep everyone happy, you may have to split up the holidays, going to Thanksgiving at one home and Christmas or Hanukkah at the other. You might switch the celebrations every other year.

The rub comes at celebrations you will probably want to have at your home, like birthday parties or graduations. If grandparents want to be involved, it gets very tricky if they can't stand to be in the same room together or if they feel that they are competing for the child's attention with the other set of grandparents. Some neurotic grandparents are not capable of keeping the child as the focus of the celebration if their "rivals" are present. You will probably have to have separate celebration times or days to avoid collisions.

Difficulties get stickier when parents age and you end up hosting most of the holiday events and family celebrations. Your children will have become busier and less flexible about having two separate celebrations for every occasion, and you may not have the energy you once had to do all the juggling of schedules. You may have to have the talk you've been dreading for years, explain the necessity for having only one celebration, invite them both to attend, and, having asked them to help you make it a pleasant time for the sake of whomever's celebration it is, let them decide whether to come.

This may all seem like it is too far in the future to consider, and it may seem that I am painting a rather grim picture. Unfortunately, such family conflicts are more frequent than you might think. Many in-laws do not like each other, for a variety of rational and irrational reasons. Many parents place their adult children in no-win positions. Many think that the newly married couple should do all of the adjusting to them, and do not consider how they could help the situation. Learning to get past these challenges will be one of the most interesting, frustrating, and difficult accomplishments of your marriage.

If you and your intended have a good idea that your parents will not get along together, now is the time to plan how you will handle some of the inevitable conflicts that could arise. You will learn a lot about your intended by talking some of this through. How sensitive is he or she about the relationships involved? How defensive is he or she about their parents? How willing is he or she to take charge of talking to their parents, and working out plans with you to avoid difficulties? If your intended is unhelpful before you are married, don't count on them being helpful later. Do you want to do battle alone?

Question 10. How close you will be living to your in-laws will be important, whether you get along with them or not, and whether they get along with each other or not. If you do not get along with a set of in-laws, it helps to have the contact as infrequent as possible. Ideally, you would have the in-laws you like best living closest to you. But even that does not guarantee that all will go smoothly.

I ran into Jackie after a Sunday school teachers' meeting. She had seemed rather distracted at the meeting, so I asked how things were going. The story came tumbling out as if a dam had burst. Jackie and Bill were experiencing their annual bout of anxiety and frustration. Thanksgiving was two days away and his parents were coming from across the country for their annual appearance. They always arrived at rush hour on Thanksgiving eve at one of the busiest airports in the world. Bill had a responsibility for the company award reception that was always given before Thanksgiving in order to avoid the Christmas party season, which meant that she would have to pack up the kids and battle traffic to pick his parents up.

"It's not like they couldn't come any time they wished. They're retired, for Heaven's sake!" she said. "And then they will say, 'Fish and visitors smell in three days,' and leave on Saturday, missing the kids' program on Sunday." She was getting more wound up as she continued. "I don't know why they bother comming at all. They will lecture the kids. They don't seem to know how to be grandparents. It will be three days of chaos and everyone in our family will only be relieved when they are gone."

"Have you talked about their coming at a better time, or staying longer?" I asked. "It's like talking to a brick wall," Jackie replied. "And Bob has always had problems talking to them. He says arguing with them is just too painful." She parted, saying they would just have to put up with it. It was apparent she had really married into a dysfunctional family, and her only help was that their contacts were only once a year.

If you will be living close to only one set of parents, be aware that the other set will feel left out. It will be necessary to make regular phone calls, e-mail, or letter contact if you want closeness. Sending videotapes or tapes of programs can help bridge the miles. But it is not all up to you. Hopefully you will have parents that want to keep up the contact.

Question 11. I hope the answer to this is no. You will not find any counselor who thinks this is a good idea, but they often will not say why. Stop and think about it. Any time a child goes back to living in his or her own home, it is very difficult for them not to revert to the role they had as a child in that family. And it is very hard for parents not to treat them as a child. Since you both will be depending on them for housing and meals, they will treat you as dependents instead of equals. You will feel obligated to do things with them and do things their way.

Aside from that, you will not have the privacy you need to work out the differences or conflicts you may have. As thoughtful and helpful as parents may try to be, they probably will give you advice if you seem to need it, and will give more help than you would be getting if you were on your own. You will not be functioning as a normal couple if you are under their roof.

Having said this, I know that there are some circumstances in which living with parents may be a necessity. If this is the case, it should be for as brief a time as possible, and you need to discuss some ground rules with them ahead of time. Such simple items as bed times, bathroom schedules, where and when cars are to be parked, and laundry may seem trivial, but they can cause real resentments if not worked out beforehand. Interaction with other children is potentially a real problem, especially if you get a room they were planning on using. Some thought to these issues, and getting them clear in advance, will help make this transitional phase of your marriage successful. Otherwise, these can become the worst days of your lives.

Question 12. How important it is to you and your intended to have good relations with your in-laws will determine how much effort you put into making it happen, and how successful you will be. In general, wives turn out to be the ones who do the most to make such relations work. But if relationships are important to a husband, he should be prepared to help do the scheduling, house-cleaning, and parenting necessary to make visits and celebrations as good as possible. If your intended tells you it is important but says it is up to you to make the relationship work, believe that he or she means it. Decide right now whether you think that will work for you. I anticipate that there will be a lot of resentment ahead.

Like every other undertaking in your married life, managing all of the relationships involved will be best done if together you agree about what you are doing. It also helps to know ahead of time what kind of people you will be dealing with. If they aren't healthy emotionally, your job will be much harder. Unfortunately, the seemingly right person for you may not come equipped with the greatest parents. If they are really dysfunctional, you should have second thoughts about their child. Has he or she dealt with the damage that resulted from being brought up by these parents? If so, that is good. If not, stop and get help before you go any further. This is especially true if you suspect that they are alcoholics, addicts, or mentally ill.

I hope these questions have given you some helpful insights to think about. There is more to being married than you may have thought. But do not fear; there is a right person with a good family out there just waiting for you!

Chapter 10

Can We Talk?!?

For by your words you will be acquitted, and by your words you will be condemned.

Jesus of Nazareth, Matthew 12:37

It is practically impossible to distinguish between real listening and love.

Paul Tournier

Communication is the name of the game in marriage, it's been said—and said so often that we've almost forgotten what it means. More accurately, it should be said that good communication is the name of the game, for not all communication is helpful or healthy. Just because you are talking, screaming, fighting, or cuddling does not mean you are communicating well!

I remember a story that my childhood pastor told about a young couple who came to him for premarital counseling. He asked them if they had talked about several subjects like money, children, where they would live, etc., and got no response. Finally, he asked them what they did talk about when they were together. The two looked at him like he was from some other planet, and said "Talk?!" He decided that they had been too busy studying anatomy to do much talking.

As you have gathered by now, talking about things ahead of time is crucial to making a successful choice of a marriage partner, as well as making a successful marriage. But just talking is not all there is to communication. Listening is equally important.

In this chapter I will point you toward ways of communicating that will help you in all phases of your marriage. But first the question: Just how well do you communicate now?

Plenty of good books exist to help people communicate better in their marriage, bearing witness to the great need for couples to do a better job. I'll list some in the Bibliography. But why not do a bit of reality checking before you take the plunge? For if you are not communicating well before you get married, what makes you think it will improve later? Here are some good questions to help you evaluate communication in your relationship. *(Circle answers)*

1. Are you a better talker or a listener?
   Talker   Listener   Don't know
   Is your prospective mate a better talker or listener?
   Talker   Listener   Don't know
   (If either question results in a Don't know, ask your family or their friends)

2. Does your prospective mate avoid conflict at all costs when talking with you or others?   Yes   No   Some of the time   Most of the time   Almost always

3. How have you handled disagreements? *(Check all that apply)*
   __ One of us leaves in the middle of an argument
   __ One of us gets our way by crying or pouting
   __ One of us slams the door and walks out

___ We never raise our voices
___ One of us may leave the room to calm down but comes back and talks later
___ We talk things through until we reach a conclusion
___ We never have any disagreements
___ One of us solves things by never admitting there is a problem
___ One of us is always the one who gives in

4. Can you express your feelings to your potential mate without him/her becoming defensive?
    Yes   No   Sometimes   Rarely
    Can you express your feelings to your potential mate without becoming defensive yourself?
    Yes   No   Sometimes   Rarely

5. What do you talk about most of the time? (*Check any but circle the major ones*)
    ___ Work   ___ Parties   ___ Drinking
    ___ Sports   ___ Clothes   ___ Drugs
    ___ Other people ___ Future plans   ___ School
    ___ Sex   ___ Feelings   ___ Likes/dislikes
    ___ Money   ___ Children
    ___ Common hobbies, interests
    ___ His/her interests or hobbies
    ___ Other_____

6. Is your prospective mate's talk mostly positive or negative?
    Positive   Negative

7. Do you feel manipulated, controlled, or put down in your talk with him/her?
    Yes   No   Sometimes   Rarely   Often
    Do you feel like you can never win?
    Yes   No   Sometimes   Rarely   Often

Comments

Question 1. Are you a better talker than a listener? You may not be the best judge of this! In my experience, people who say they are good listeners are often the worst listeners. Ask your parents, your friends, and your prospective mate this question and you may get a better idea. Listening is an art. It does not mean that you listen just long enough to know where to break in with your opinion or story. Listening involves hearing both what the person says and what they mean. **Communicating means hearing the person long enough so that you understand both the words and the emotional content of what they are saying, and then letting them know you understand by what you say back to them.**

You might want to re-read that definition. What passes for much of our daily interchange with others is not really communication. People say things and receive replies, not realizing that the other person has not heard what was meant. Neither person listens with full attention. Sometimes that doesn't matter. But perhaps it explains why so often on our job or in our everyday dealings with people there is so much misunderstanding and miscommunication. In marriage, if one of you is a poor listener or a constant talker, small problems will rapidly become major conflicts. If you have already had arguments in which you felt the other person just wasn't "getting it," it is a good sign that at least one of you isn't listening well.

It is important to know that men and women do not listen or talk in the same way (a notion that gave rise to the ideas in the *Men are from Mars, Women are from Venus* books). Women tend to be better listeners and tend to be better at hearing the emotional content of a statement. They tend to be better at expressing their feelings, but often do not say directly what they mean. Men tend to say what they mean and tend to hear the rational or factual content of a statement. They are not very good at hearing the emotional content of a statement or expressing feelings verbally.

All this leads to some very interesting exchanges, like when a husband smelling something burning on the stove announces to his wife, "The steak is burnt." His wife bursts into tears because she thinks she hears him saying: "I hate your cooking!" If pressed, he would say, "All I said (and meant) was that the steak was burnt." But she would say she was hearing what he meant, not what he said.

Such miscommunication is normal between men and women, and nearly every couple has to learn how to hear each other better. Men have to realize that what she is most likely to hear is what she thinks is the emotional content of what he is saying, and to be sure to let her know what he really means. Women need to learn that not everything he says has some emotional content or personal attack attached. They need to listen first to the rational content of his statement. Of course, this learning is easier if the relationship is built on emotional maturity, trust, and love. Otherwise, we have what has been termed the Battle of the Sexes, but what is really mostly a communication gap.

The transactional analysis movement, popularized in Thomas Harris's book, *I'm OK, You're OK,* pointed out that each communication between two people is a transaction whose meaning reveals the emotional state of the person making it. Without going into the whole theory, which is still well worth exploring, the statement a person makes comes from "tapes" of unexamined rules, emotions, and assumptions. These tapes contain rules learned from ones parents or authority figures, emotions (often feelings of inferiority or powerlessness) experienced as a child, or rational assessments of facts based on adult reasoning. Child tapes contain feelings of "I'm not OK, You're OK" (inferiority), or "I'm not OK, You're not OK" (depression). Parent tapes contain the manipulation of not OK feelings that says "I'm OK, You're not OK." Adult statements are based on feelings that say "I'm OK, You're OK."

The problem of communication is that a statement may be coming from all three tapes, and the person responding will be affected by the emotional state they are in. Harris's classic example is of a husband who comes home hot and tired from a frustrating day on the job. He heads for the refrigerator, grabs a bottle of beer, and begins rummaging in the drawer for a bottle opener. When he can't find it, he says to his wife, "Where did you hide the bottle opener, dear?"

Of course, this is a loaded statement. His wife hears the punishing content of the statement (the hook or invitation to an argument) that is contained in the word "hide." (Parent: "If I kept my business the way you keep our house, we'd be sunk!") She hears the Child underneath the statement ("I'm hot, tired, and thirsty and I can't get a break.") and she hears an Adult requesting information ("Where is the bottle opener?"). To which one will she respond?

That will largely depend on how she is feeling, and whether she is spoiling for a fight. If she is feeling depressed ("I'm not OK, You're not OK") and hopeless after a trying day, she may just burst into tears and leave for the bedroom. If she is a little more healthy, but still feeling stepped on ("I'm not OK, You're OK"), she might say, "I try my best to keep things nice, but with three little kids, there is no way I can please you. Why can't you help?" Either response, and the missed communication that follows, ought to be enough to ruin their evening.

If she is feeling tired and also a bit angry after a trying day, and hears only the challenge in the statement, she could respond with a Parent ("I'm OK, You're not OK") statement of her own, like, "Why don't you take off your muddy boots before you track mud all over my clean floor, you jerk." This could start a battle that could last for days. Note that she has responded to the perceived content of the statement, that is, what she thinks he meant, but not to the feelings underneath it or the request for information.

Or she could say, "I hid it right next to the napkins, dear." Now that is an Adult ("I'm OK, You're OK") response. She has done three things. She has let him know that she heard the Parental "hook," but is not about to be dragged into an argument over a bottle opener. She also dealt with the Child feelings underneath the statement. She pats the Child on the head, in essence, and tells it everything is going to be all-right (the bottle opener is not lost). Finally, she conveys to the Adult the information it wanted, which was the location of the opener. She thus ends the argument before it begins.

Learning these important insights into how what we say tells us about what our transactions really mean has helped many people. Just getting them to analyze where their statements are coming from for a couple of weeks is often enough to get them switched on to the Adult track and improve their patterns of communication.

Another important difference in the way men and women talk occurs when they are "discussing" or arguing about something. Women tend to try to clarify their feelings, so they talk more in an attempt to resolve the discomfort. Men tend to clam up when faced with a conflict. This only makes the woman more uncomfortable, so she will talk even more. The argument accelerates until he finally tells her to shut up. Many wives' chief complaint about their husbands is that "He won't talk to me!" while husbands complain that "She never stops talking!"

Learning to communicate around this basic difference takes new skills, especially the one of understanding that men and women tend to talk for different reasons. Men tend to communicate in order to exchange information, ideas, or solve problems. Women tend to communicate in order to share feelings or nurture relationships. This explains how two women can be talking simultaneously, filling in each other's sentences and conversing happily, seemingly understanding everything the other says—a process that baffles men completely.

It also explains how men can talk for hours about baseball scores, philosophy, or politics, but become completely tongue-tied when trying to talk about feelings. When a woman confronts a man about something in their relationship, he will sense that it is either a problem that he needs to fix, or that he is being attacked. In either case, he will often resort to silence when he can't seem to fix the problem, or he will leave the argument to get away from the threatening feelings involved. This leaves the woman feeling unheard and frustrated. Using the "I Feel" formula is one way of avoiding this impasse. (See comment under Question 4 below.)

Getting back to the original question: If you are both talkers, you will probably find that you will be starving for someone to listen to you after awhile. If you both listen well, you will probably communicate well. By this I don't mean that either of you are so painfully shy that you don't talk at all. Communication takes two. If you marry the strong, silent type, he won't necessarily get more communicative later on. If you marry the shy wallflower, she may not be able to talk openly about what she needs. Both can learn to communicate, but realize that it will take a lot of work. You should start by taking time now to do some listening and talking together.

If, in the process, you learn that one or both of you has difficulty accurately communicating feelings or hearing what the other is saying, counseling can help. Psychologists or pastoral counselors can help you with normal communication problems. If something deeper is revealed, such as an abusive background, they will probably refer you to a psychotherapist. At any rate, now is a good time to deal with whatever the problem is. Otherwise, you will not have the tools to build a successful marriage.

Question 2: This is a crucial question. If your potential mate is a conflict-avoider, he or she may appear to get along well with you and others, but it is at a cost to him or her and you that may well undo your marriage later on. For one thing, such pleasers may swallow a lot of rage by always bending over backward to avoid conflict with others, and that rage can come back at you in several ways.

The person may actually make himself or herself sick, because this avoidance is very stressful, or they may simply be very uncommunicative with you. In the worst case they may take out their anger on you with physical or mental abuse. They may not be able to handle stressful demands of marriage and family and may become irresponsible about money, parenting, or work. I covered some of this in Chapter 1 under the heading of emotional maturity.

If your potential mate is always agreeing with your point of view or your suggestions when you suspect that he or she actually disagrees, or if they give in to you or friends to keep the peace, but later let you know they didn't want to, or if they get talked into doing things for others a lot when they should be doing something else, you are seeing a conflict avoider. Everybody does these things once in awhile. But if this is a consistent pattern of behavior, you are going to have serious problems later on. Now is a good time to talk about it and get some professional help. If the person comes from an alcoholic or abusive background, long-term help will be needed, because this is often a symptom of codependency. (See Chapter 2)

Question 3: If you have had no disagreements or arguments, is it because you really have the same ideas, or because you haven't done much talking? Some conflict is inevitable in every relationship, simply because the two of you come from different backgrounds and different family systems that you regard as normal and right. How you handle these differences will make your marriage stronger or tear it apart. So how are you doing now?

If you checked any of the first three choices (leaving in the middle of an argument, slamming the door and walking out, or crying or pouting to get one's way), they are sure signs of emotional immaturity and sure signs that you will have a great deal of frustrating conflict ahead. Any time someone walks out in the middle of an argument, or slams the door and leaves, the other person is left hugely frustrated, devastated, or both. They didn't get to say all they wanted to say, but the person who left got the last word without saying anything.

Like crying or pouting to get one's way, walking out is a form of emotional blackmail. All of these tactics may end the argument in the short run, but the victim ends up feeling cheated, helpless, or like they can never win. In essence, the fight was not fair, the issues are usually left unresolved, and the feelings will erupt later in some other way, either in a future argument or in some other destructive behavior.

There are rules for a fair fight in marriage (Charlie Shedd, in his classic book *Letters to Philip,* lists seven) and these behaviors violate several of them. If you or your prospective mate indulges in them now, either get some help now in learning how to communicate better or resign yourself to some very rocky times ahead. You may see marriages around you that survive even though the couples play such games, but they are not the best marriages. And don't you want the best?

If you checked any of the next three choices, you are on the right track. If you can discuss things without raising your voices, you are pretty rare, but it really does help to keep the argument rational if you lower your voice instead of raising the threat level. To keep the debate constructive means to realize that not every argument needs to be won. Not every suggestion by the other person is a personal attack on your values. And just because your family did things one way doesn't mean it's the only way something can be done.

It is always permissible to call for a time-out to let one or the other of you calm down, as long as you both agree to it. And you should agree to it as long as you both understand that this does not mean you are through discussing the subject for good. The best way is to discuss something until you have reached some kind of a resolution. The resolution can be that you agree on a solution (for instance, instead of arguing because one of you squeezes from the middle of the tube while the other rolls it neatly from the bottom, you agree to buy two tubes of toothpaste), that you agree to disagree, or that you agree that you have talked enough for now and want to talk about it later.

If you checked that you never have any disagreements, do a reality check. Are you talking about anything important? Are you still on such tentative ground in the relationship that you are afraid to disagree? Maybe you need to launch a discussion on something controversial just to see how you handle it. If you have discussed some very important values and are very much agreed on them, great. But make sure you are not just avoiding subjects because you are afraid to disagree.

If you checked either of the last two responses, you are in for real trouble. One way of avoiding conflict is simply to deny that there is any. This borders on real mental illness. It is at best a kind of denial that leaves the other person baffled or defeated. At worst it will lead to other kinds of denial and irresponsible behavior. The kind of mental gymnastics required to keep up this front pushes people over the edge. It often goes along with alcohol and drug abuse. The spouse of such a person is often confused by the denial, then may sometimes conclude it is their fault for feeling that there really is a problem (especially if the denier keeps suggesting that the spouse is the one with the problem). If this sounds like you, get help immediately. Be prepared to end the relationship if the other person will not get help. They are usually so deep in denial that they won't.

If you find that one of you always gives in to settle an argument, you need to ask why. If it is you, are you so afraid of losing the other person's love that you can't be yourself or have your own opinions or values? If so, be aware that no lasting relationship can be built on fabrication. Sooner or later, he or she is going to find out that you are different from the front you are putting up. If your prospective mate does not love you for who you are, who does he or she love? Do you want to keep up a false image of yourself forever?

What will happen when he or she does discover the real you? Wouldn't it be better to find out now, rather than later? It is time for a good talk. Couples are often so busy and stressed trying to impress each other that they are very relieved when they find out that they don't need to do so. Successful couples are comfortable with who they are, and feel comfortable just being themselves with each other. If you can't do this now, the eventual disappointment will kill your marriage later. How many divorced people say, "He or she just wasn't the person I thought I married"? Far too many.

Are you so unsure of yourself, or so overwhelmed by the other person's superior knowledge or personality, that you don't question their opinions or values? You (or your intended, if they are the one who always gives in) may have a lot of insecurity, or a lot of emotional immaturity to deal with before you are ready for marriage. You need to feel like you are competent, lovable, and worthwhile, with values and opinions that matter, before you can successfully be a partner with someone else. If you don't, you will submerge yourself in the other person's personality and lose your own.

Even if your partner is smarter or more outstanding in his or her field than you, you should feel enough value as a person that you are sure you can be a partner for him or her. If you do not, you will end up saying, "I don't know who I am anymore," and your mate will say, "We grew apart; he or she just became boring and a drag all the time." Translation: "I met someone a lot more interesting at the office!" In '90s terminology, you both need to get a life before you can make one together.

There is another danger. If you are so completely overwhelmed by another person, you are a perfect setup for an abusive relationship. The abuser will sense that here is someone that he or she can easily control and bully. All he or she has to do is remind you of how stupid you are and how smart they are to cow you into doing whatever they want. The more you give in to them, the less they respect you and the less you respect yourself, and the less able you become to get out of this terrible situation. If you sense any of this developing, **get out now!** (See Chapter 13).

Question 4: How well are you able to communicate how you feel without you or your potential mate getting defensive? If you have difficulty because he or she doesn't accept your feelings as valid or worthwhile, you've got trouble. If he or she is threatened by your feelings, or even by discussing feelings, communication is going to be difficult, if not impossible. You need to sort out with a counselor what is happening in order to know if this is a problem you can do something about or if it is an indicator of a deep-seated problem.

One thing to know is that, in general, men have more trouble talking about and dealing with feelings than women do. They especially have a hard time when women express negative feelings or feelings that seem to demand a response (like commitment). If the statement of your feelings comes off as a personal attack, they will withdraw rather than communicate. All couples can learn a way around this communications trap. In his book *The "I Feel" Formula,* Robert Ball suggests that you learn to express feelings by saying, "When you say (or do) _____ it makes me feel like _____." The reason behind this is that how you feel is not debatable, and you have a right to your feelings. The statement is not a direct attack upon the other person, and it allows them to either clarify or explain what they really meant.

So for instance you might say, "When you didn't introduce me to your friends it made me feel like I'm not important to you." It gives him or her a chance to say, "Oh, I'm sorry, I didn't mean to make you feel that way, but I couldn't think of their names so I didn't want to embarrass myself by introducing them." This could give you a chance to say, "Let's work out a signal so that I can introduce myself and save you the embarrassment." Note that the argument stopped before it ever got started. The offender was able to clarify his actions without being threatened, and a solution was reached to prevent future misunderstandings. That is good communication.

Other writers have slightly different versions of this formula, but it really does work. The way to keep an expression of feelings from developing into a destructive argument is to keep focused on the issue or feelings involved and not let it get into personal attacks. You may feel like saying, "You are a real jerk" but you will get a lot further by saying something about how his or her behavior made you feel.

Arguments, as opposed to real communication, are about who is right or wrong, who is to blame, or who has the power. Nobody wins in the long run when you argue, and feelings are the first casualty. If you can get differences and disagreements resolved without destructive arguments by using the "I Feel" technique, you will have a far happier relationship.

If you try this approach and still don't get any response, or get a put-down or a rejoinder that implies that you don't have any right to feel the way you do, you should not ignore the fact that you have a real problem. You will either need to get some professional help in learning to communicate or let this relationship end. If your intended mate is making you feel like you are on the defensive, or if they just won't deal with you or get help, this problem will not get better and it could get much worse. This is not the right person for you.

Question 5: So what do you talk about most of the time, assuming you do talk and don't just sit in front of the television or go to movies? The more issues you discuss, especially those I've mentioned in this book, the better. But just because there is a lot of talk going on does not mean it is meaningful communication. Pay attention to who is doing most of the talking. Is it you? Does that mean the other person is really listening, or are they simply replying with grunts or monosyllables? What you talk about most may give you a clue to what is most important to you or your mate.

Remember that males will tend to find it easier to talk about work, sports, and hobbies than feelings. Females will tend to talk easily about feelings, other people, and likes and dislikes. If one or the other of you talks only about things in their comfort zone, it is a sign that either they aren't sure enough of your relationship to get out of it, or they may not be emotionally mature enough to get beyond "small talk."

You'd better try deliberately moving on to one of the less safe subjects and find out where you stand. You can be straightforward about this without being threatening. You can say, "You know, I love the way you know all about every baseball player that ever lived, and I like talking about it with you, but I'd also like to know how you feel about your family and how you would like a family to be [or some other subject]." If he or she can't or won't deal with such a subject after a few tactful tries, then you probably have an emotionally immature person or at least a very poor communicator on your hands. Do you want either of those qualities in a mate? I hope your answer is no.

If most of your talk together centers around drinking, drugs, or parties, you are identifying a problem that is even more dangerous in the long run. If most of your talk is about these things, or if most of your prospective mate's talk is centered around when the next party is or where or when they will get another drink or hit, one of you has or will have a serious alcohol or drug problem. Go back to Chapter 2 and review what you found there and the comments. You need to get help, get out, or both. You are not ready to get married or start a serious relationship if this is the center of your world.

If your talk is centered mostly on sex, you need to evaluate. If most of your talk is simply a prelude to getting what you or your mate wants out of the other, you may well be simply using each other, or mistaking sex for love. It is normal for you to be sexually attracted to someone, but if all of the romantic talk and passion leaves either one of you feeling used or wondering if that is all the other person wants, now is a good time to stop and find out.

So many of the letters in advice columns complain that, while the sex is great, he or she won't commit to marriage, or won't talk about anything else, or doesn't have anything else in common. It does not take a rocket scientist to figure out that they should have been talking and getting to know each other before they ended up in bed. It goes almost without saying that if one of you feels like you are merely a sex object for the other, you probably are. Now is the time to decide if that is what you want to be.

Question 6: This question is a good check for personality traits that may turn out to be major problems later. If your talk is mostly positive, this is a good sign of emotional maturity and long-term compatibility. If you marked negative, are you dealing with a whiner, moody, or irritable person, a person who is extremely needy, or a person who always seems to be having bad luck or being hurt?

It is possible that you are involved with someone who is just involved in an unhappy or difficult situation right now, which is temporary. But if you can look back and see that the person often or always seems to be in difficulties, or that there is a pattern to their unhappiness or negativity, you are dealing with emotional immaturity, personality disorders, or behavioral problems. Ask their friends or family members. If they indicate that they are always in a jam or often moody, you have a good indication that this is not the right mate for you, unless, of course, you like to be around moody or needy people! In that case, you need help.

Question 7: You may have observed that I have asked this question before in a different way. If you answered Yes or even Sometimes to either part of the question, you are dealing with a manipulative, possibly cruel or even abusive person. **Get out of this relationship now!** You should never have to feel put down by someone who says they love you. Love does not put another person down or degrade them.

The longer you stay around this person, the more you will be encouraging their behavior, and the more likely you will be to accept it. If you need help to get out of the relationship, get it; but act now! (See Chapter 13.) Most people who have been involved in abusive relationships have reported that it began with abusive communication and that they should have seen it coming. Unfortunately, many people do not survive abusive relationships or end up going back to them until serious injury or death is the result. Don't be a victim. You may not feel like it, but you do deserve better.

So, high on your list of qualities to look for in a mate is the ability to communicate openly and maturely with you. Don't settle for less. The quality of your marriage depends on it. Press on! There is one more set of major issues to deal with on your way to discovering the right someone for you.

Chapter 11

Religious and Cultural Differences

Religion is the individual's attitude toward God and man as expressed in faith, in worship, in life and in service.
Charles Foster Kent

I would not give much for your religion unless it can be seen. Lamps do not talk, but they do shine.
Charles Haddon Spurgeon

When I first started in ministry, I found a statistic that I would quote to couples about to get married. It was that 1 out of 4 marriages would end in divorce if the couple were twenty-one or older when they married. Couples under twenty-one faced only a fifty percent chance of having a successful marriage. But, if a couple had a religious faith in common, their odds of failure dropped to only 1 in 117. And if the couple practiced their faith, praying together, attending worship, and became involved in their faith community, their odds of success skyrocketed: Only 1 in 1169 of such marriages would end in divorce.

Those statistics have changed in the last thirty years, and not for the better. But the fact is that marriages held together by the force of a common religious faith and practice still have a much better chance of succeeding than those that are not. Religion is powerful glue. For one thing, when a couple asks for God's help in their everyday life, there will be a resource beyond themselves to help when things get rough. For another, when a couple takes seriously the vows they made before God, there is a special sacred fence around that marriage that our society in general no longer provides.

Religion can and should be one of the forces that hold your relationship together, but, if you do not share religious values, it can also be one of the factors that drive a couple apart. The reason for this is that religion shapes your values and identity at a very deep level. Even if you profess to have no religion, this is still a religious identity and it shapes your values and lifestyle. "Every man, either to his terror or to his consolation, has some sense of religion," said James Harrington. Shared values, especially religious values and practices, will hold a marriage together. Unshared values will drive a wedge between you.

Denise and Ted sat on the couch in my office for their premarital counseling session. Denise attended our church somewhat irregularly; Ted was a Roman Catholic. He had been married briefly to a woman who had left him for someone younger, someone who was around more than Ted's shipping business allowed. Since he was divorced, the Catholic Church would not allow him to be married in his church unless he undertook a long and expensive annulment process which he regarded as hypocritical.

I ended up doing a lot of such marriages, partly because our church was the one place such couples could come. Sometimes the local priests, who were bound by the policies but didn't agree with them, would come and assist in the weddings. Most of the time, the last time I would see the couple was at the wedding. For many, the fact that the Catholic partner was not allowed to take communion and hadn't been allowed to marry there meant that they really didn't feel welcome in their own church, and the non-Catholic spouse decided to make religion a non-issue in their family by ignoring it.

Ted didn't seem a lot different. He was pretty bitter about his church's stand. But as we talked, Denise indicated that she wanted to join our church, and Ted said that in spite of his bad experience he wanted their children to grow up in church. He said he had to be gone a lot and often would not be home on weekends. In fact, he knew he was asking Denise to do the lion's share of raising children, but they had discussed that and she wanted to do so. The choice of religious upbringing would be up to her.

They got married and Denise became a member. I didn't see her often at church, but one day she came in and requested to have their new baby baptized. She was more regular in attendance after that and eventually got more active in church. I rarely saw Ted, but she told me of his travels, on which she occasionally accompanied him. She did what many spouses of mixed marriages do. She practiced her faith alone and made sure that her child was raised in the faith. It seemed like a lonely road, but at least one of them had found a way to bridge a gap that could have been divisive. They didn't seem to have the faith in common that would have strengthened their marriage, but she held it together with faith and tenacity.

As religious values are either unifying or divisive, the same is true of cultural and ethnic backgrounds. They are a deep part of who you and your potential mate are. In America we tended to downplay such differences, continued to blend cultures in our "melting pot," up through the '60s. But these days there is a movement to celebrate differences and recapture our roots. Whether this is a good or bad thing for American society in the long run, it appears to be preserving ethnic and cultural differences and making them more significant than ever.

The importance of all of this for you is that, in spite of the media's attempts to show all kinds of family and ethnic groupings as normal, the blended families and sitcom groupings you see on TV are caricatures at best. They ignore the realities of dealing with real religious and cultural differences in a marriage. If you marry across religious or cultural/ethnic lines, you may be able to make a successful marriage, but there are a lot of barriers to cross. And in general, the more different the religious or ethnic backgrounds are, the more difficult it will be for you (and your families) to adjust to each other and make it work.

While it has been said that opposites attract, and there is research to show that this is true, opposites do not necessarily make the best marriage partners. The more major differences there are in important areas of your life, the harder it is to overcome them. And this is especially true for religious differences, even more so when the religious group is also an ethnic or racial group (Arab Moslems, Russian Jews, Greek Orthodox Christians, Vietnamese Buddhists, etc.).

When you have to negotiate language and cultural barriers as well as religious differences, you have many more possibilities for misunderstandings and resentments to develop. Again, a marriage can survive, but it takes a lot of work, a lot of flexibility, and a lot of understanding on all sides to make it work. Since there are plenty of challenges in married life anyhow, do you want to add these additional burdens to your marriage?

If you and your prospective mate are of different religious and/or racial/ethnic backgrounds, now is the time to analyze and talk about how those differences will affect your marriage and family life. Even if the differences do not seem major, the following questions will help you determine your likelihood of success.

First, list your and your prospective mate's religious and ethnic information:

Religion, Denomination, Nationality/Ethnic group, Race
Yours_____
His\hers_____

[Note: *Religion* means major religious group: Christianity, Judaism, Buddhism, Islam, Hinduism, Jainism, Sikhism, Confucianism, Taoism, Shintoism, Zoroastrianism, or B'hai. *Denomination* means a branch of a religion, such as Roman Catholic, Presbyterian, or Baptist denominations of Christianity; Sunni or Shiite branches of Islam; or Nichiren or Zen branches of Buddhism. For the purpose of this questionnaire, list Jehovah's

Witnesses, Mormonism, and Christian Science as denominations under Christianity. List New Age under Hinduism.]

(Circle answers where applicable)

1. How important is your faith to you?
    Very important   Somewhat important   Unimportant

    How important is it to your prospective mate?
    Very important   Somewhat important   Unimportant

2. Does he or she:
    Attend worship services?
    Regularly   Occasionally   Rarely   Never
    Take part in Church/religious activities?
    Regularly   Occasionally   Rarely   Never
    Pray?
    Regularly   Occasionally   Rarely   Never
    Say prayers at meals?
    Regularly   Occasionally   Rarely   Never
    Talk about faith with you or others?
    Regularly   Occasionally   Rarely   Never
    Give money regularly?
    Regularly   Occasionally   Rarely   Never
    Read Scripture or religious literature?
    Regularly   Occasionally   Rarely   Never

3. Do you:
    Attend worship services?
    Regularly   Occasionally   Rarely   Never
    Take part in Church/religious activities?
    Regularly   Occasionally   Rarely   Never
    Pray?
    Regularly   Occasionally   Rarely   Never
    Say prayers at meals?
    Regularly   Occasionally   Rarely   Never
    Talk about faith with him/her or others?
    Regularly   Occasionally   Rarely   Never

Give money regularly?
Regularly   Occasionally   Rarely   Never
Read Scripture or religious literature?
Regularly   Occasionally   Rarely   Never

4.   Does his/her faith seem to influence their everyday
     behavior and ethics?
     Yes   No   Somewhat   A Lot   Not sure
     Does yours?
     Yes   No   Somewhat   A Lot   Not sure

5.   How important is it to your parents that you marry someone
     of the same faith or denomination?
     Important   Somewhat important   Not at all

     How important is it to his/her parents that they marry
     someone of the same faith or denomination?
     Important   Somewhat important   Not at all

6.   As a condition of getting married, will either of you have to
     convert to the other's religion or faith group?   Yes   No
     If yes, how do you feel about that?
     How does he/she feel?

7.   If one of you is of another faith group, are there also
     national or cultural differences that are involved? (For
     example, your fiancé is a Moslem from Lebanon)
     Yes   No
     If yes, do you have a good idea of the expectations of a wife
     or husband in that culture?

Comments

While American culture tends to blur the distinctions between
religions, there really are basic differences in the way each major
religion thinks and feels about life, death, marriage, and the way we

treat others outside our religious community. It is evident that some religions and even denominations are more compatible with others than other faiths may be. It is easier for a Liberal or Reformed Jew to marry a Christian than for any Jew to marry a Moslem, easier for a Buddhist to marry a Shintoist than a Sikh, or easier for a Baptist to marry a Presbyterian than a Mormon.

This is because some of these faiths would require that the outsider convert to their faith in order to marry, while some would actually have their family disown the child who married outside the faith. Others might allow the marriage, but treat the person who was not of their faith as an outsider and demand that the children be raised in their faith. In general, the more conservative or orthodox the faith community, the more restrictive it will be about marriage to those outside the faith. And the more different the faiths are from each other, the more difficult it will be to marry successfully across those lines.

In order to convey the level of difficulty, assign number values to the differences you discover as you write down you and your prospective mate's religious and cultural information.

__ If you are of the same religion, score 0; if different, score 1.

__ If the religions are different and are or recently have been at war with each other, (such as Jews and Moslems, Bosnian Christians and Serbian Moslems, or Sikhs and Hindus) score 2.

__ If you are of the same religion and the same denomination, score 0.

__ If you are of the same religion but different mainline denominations, score 1.

__ If the denominations are quite different, or are fringe groups or cults (see note below), score 2.

__ If either of your denominations does not recognize the other as valid, score 2.

__ If you are of the same nationality and ethnic group, score 0.

__ If you are of the same nationality but of a different ethnic group in which your languages are different, score 1.

__ If you are of different nationalities, score 1.

__ If you are of very different ethnic groups or ones that have

recently considered themselves enemies, score 2.
__ If you are the same race, score 0.
__ If you are of different races, score 1.

Total the scores. If you like, put them on a scale of 1 to 5. The score simply indicates the number of barriers you have to cross to make a successful marriage. The higher the score, the more difficult it will be.

Please note that I am not saying that marriages across religious, ethnic, or racial lines cannot work. Many have and will. But it is more difficult for several reasons. The first is that the families on both sides may find it difficult to accept such a marriage. If they are of the opinion that people should marry their own kind, or if they are prejudiced against other racial, ethnic, or religious groups, they will have to be won over and you should not minimize the difficulty of doing this.

If there is a long-standing enmity between your faith communities, like between Catholics and Protestants in Northern Ireland or Palestinian Arabs and Israeli Jews, you may find it nearly impossible to have either family accept the marriage. Unfortunately, some groups have very long memories and will not let go of past grudges. It is especially difficult if ethnic or religious groups are also political or national groups. So if you find yourself falling in love with someone of a very different cultural, religious, or racial/ethnic background, realize that you may be in for some very big adjustments. Leaving your families behind may be just one of them. If marriage to your intended means never seeing your family again, is it worth it to you? Will your intended be able to leave his or her family without resenting you?

Second, the choices you will have to make if your religion is different boil down to three. One of you may have to convert to the other's religion in order to be married in the sight of their faith. This is often the best choice since you will be united in your religious faith and will not have to argue over what faith your children will be raised. If this is a matter of crossing denominational lines within the same religion, this is a fairly easy solution.

You can choose one or the other's denomination or choose another denomination that suits you both. For instance, a Presbyterian and a Roman Catholic could both feel relatively at home in an Episcopal Church, and probably both their families could accept the compromise. But be aware that this conversion may leave one or the other of you feeling like you have lost or betrayed something very important to you, and it needs to be done voluntarily and with a lot of thought. And of course, some religious communities will not accept anything less than conversion to their faith. If you are the one that has to convert, do you really want to do so? Would you do so if you didn't have to?

The second choice is for the couple to maintain their individual faiths and practice them individually or together. I once was privileged to take part in a Golden Jubilee Mass for a couple that had kept up a Catholic-Lutheran marriage for fifty years. Both attended each other's church every Sunday; both were active in serving their churches as teachers and leaders. It was a happy marriage that had started long before such marriages were common or even recognized. But they had no children, and they apparently had no family that was against the marriage. Their arrangement was the exception rather than the rule.

I have known other families where both people practice their faith individually, but usually one practices it less regularly than the other, and there is still the question of how the children will be raised to consider. It takes extra effort to make this arrangement work. It can be done, but to what extent your religious faith unites you rather than separates you depends very much on your sensitivity and tact, and how good you are at finding compromising solutions to difficult questions.

The third choice is for neither person to practice their faith. They seem to avoid offending either family or each other in this way, and of course they avoid the question of raising their children in the other's faith. Actually, however, if either family is strong in their faith, the couple will end up disappointing one or both families, who will regard them as lapsed, or even backslidden to paganism. There will be an underlying tension anytime the family is together, especially at times when religious services like Christmas Eve coincide with a family gathering.

Even if faith seems unimportant to you right now, the issue will re-emerge when you have children. Grandparents may do their best to encourage their grandchildren to adopt their faith. So while this is the most common solution for couples who marry across religious lines, it does not resolve all difficulties, and it robs the couple of the religious faith that could make their marriage much stronger. One person may end up resenting the fact that they have given up their faith to marry. So although this seems like a viable choice, it is one that you should not make lightly.

Incidentally, Ted and Denise's story had a surprise ending. By a process about which I know few details, God moved in Ted's life. I believe that he became quite ill and was hospitalized. Denise's church prayed for him and ministered to him during that illness. He was forced to slow down and let someone else do the constant traveling. He learned to regard this as a blessing and a chance to really get to know his children. The last I heard, he joined the church and became an active member. They were at last united in their faith.

Question 1: This question and the three that follow are an attempt to assess how important religious faith is to both of you. The reason for asking is that the more important faith is to a person, the more helpful it will be in holding your marriage together if it is something you have in common, but the more divisive it may become if it is something you disagree about. The questions are also a reality check. If your prospective mate has told you that his or her religion is important (or unimportant) to them because they know that it is important to you, you can use these questions to see how important it really is.

For Question 1, note the differences in your answers, if there are any. If religious faith is important to you but not important to your prospective mate, how do you think you will feel when you want to go to church or raise your children in church school and he or she does not? How would it be if the reverse were true? Do you want to be divided over something that is deeply important to you? The closer together your answers to this question are, the better your chances that religion will not become a divisive issue. However, do the reality check in Questions 2–4, because your tendency as a couple will be to say what the other wants to hear.

Questions 2 through 4: Questions 2 and 3 are reality checks against Question 1; that is, is their religion as important or unimportant as they say it is? A majority of "Regularly" answers indicate that the person's religion is important enough to them to be regularly involved. "Occasionally" answers probably indicate some importance, while "Rarely" or "Never" answers indicate that religious faith is probably unimportant. There are exceptions, such as when a person's faith has been found by reading or some other way not connected to a religious faith community, or if there is no worship center or body of believers of their faith available. But if a person is serious about their faith, they will usually practice it in the context of a faith community. If a person says their religion is important and does not practice it in the company of others, you should question how much it really means.

If your prospective mate suddenly takes up your faith, be discerning enough to realize that you may need some time to see if this new-found faith is sincere or if it is merely a tactic to make you interested in him or her. Question 4 is a reality check for both of you. If religious faith is important to you or your mate, it should have an observable effect on everyday behavior or ethical choices. No one is perfect, but does their faith make them a better person, or does it seem to have little or no influence? If it does not seem to make a difference, you should question whether it is sincere. Then ask yourself if that is going to matter to you in the long run. It should.

One final thought: if you go into a marriage thinking that you are going to convert your mate to your faith later on, you will be making a big mistake. You will probably do all of the coercive and manipulative things that people have done for centuries. Your mate will convert, if he or she does at all, only voluntarily, and usually in response to someone or something you do not expect. So anything you do beyond praying silently and being the best practitioner of your faith you can be (which is, after all, the best advertisement for your faith), will usually drive a wedge into your marriage rather than strengthening it. It may be a very long process. I knew a woman who prayed daily for seventeen years for her husband to become a Christian. He finally did, but it was not, he says, because of anything she did. If it is important to you that your mate is of the same faith, you should marry someone of your own faith. The scriptures of most major religions urge you to do so.

Question 5: If either set of parents is adamant about your marrying within the same faith, you are starting out your marriage with one very large strike against you if you go against their wishes. Remember that you and your prospective mate will have to deal with them as parents and grandparents for a long time. If your faiths are very different or have a history of enmity toward each other, this may be an especially hard thing for them to accept.

Parents have been known to have heart attacks or strokes (or at least threaten to have them) when such a marriage has been proposed. In some cases, parents have disowned children for stepping outside their faith. In some Moslem countries, a public burial is held for someone who converts or marries an infidel. How much of this do you want to be responsible for? If either one of you has to cut all ties to parents in order to marry, there is a good chance one of you will resent it, sooner or later.

If parents are not completely opposed, you will want to make sure that they accept you or your prospective mate as a person and that they see his or her religion as less important than the fact that this is a great match for their son or daughter. This will require tact, patience, and some forethought as to how you will explain how you will handle religious differences within your proposed marriage. So, of course, now is a very good time to talk about all this with your intended. It will be helpful if both of you have talked this through and if both of you talk about your plans with your parents together. Parents will respond better if you are united and give them well-thought-out answers together.

Question 6: If you answered yes, now is the time for some soul-searching. If you are the one who will be converting, make sure you understand the faith you will be embracing. You should convert because you believe in what the religion believes, not just go through the motions in order to fulfill the requirements to marry. Unless, of course, you are doing this with the intention of not practicing the faith later on and your prospective mate knows and agrees with that. Beginning your marriage with such a deception for the sake of keeping peace with parents might work in the short run, but, like most deceptions, this may really backfire later on. This is the stuff of which sitcoms are made, but they are not funny to the people that are in them.

If you find yourself having reservations about what the faith believes, get a second opinion. Talk to someone knowledgeable in your own faith community, like a minister or rabbi, who will clarify the differences and similarities for you. Make sure you know what you are agreeing to believe and what the demands of that faith will be for you and your children. Will you be comfortable with them years from now?

Be advised that in every faith there are "brand X" practitioners, cults, and sects. An entire faith should not be judged by its worst teachers or leaders but by its best. If you have reservations, is it because this leader does not practice what he or she preaches? If so, and if this is the leader your prospective mate is involved with, suggest that you both look for another church or leader. Otherwise, you will never be comfortable in that faith and it will become a divisive issue in your marriage.

Every religion has cults. These are communities that fall loosely under the belief system of one of the major faiths, but depart in enough important points from the faith that they are not considered part of them. They are characterized by having a strong leader who interprets what the group must believe, some special word or scripture that is not part of the recognized scriptural base of the religion, a rejection of some of the main teachings of the faith, and a belief that anyone not of their particular version of the faith is damned or doomed.

They are also often characterized by demands for strict loyalty to the leader or the teachings of the leader, fanaticism, and submission of the individual to the will of the group. Some use brainwashing techniques to program their followers, many demand that group members turn over their money and goods to the group or the leader. If you find that *any* of these things are true of the faith to which you are being asked to convert, get out fast. If your prospective mate is involved in a cult, attempt to get him or her to leave, but don't get sucked into it yourself. There is a lot of good religion out there but there is nothing worse than being entrapped in the bad. I will add a list of some of the recognized cults in the appendices.

Question 7: If you answered yes to this question, be aware that there are a lot of things to ask questions about before you marry someone of another culture, especially if you are a woman. There are a lot of cultures that do not have the same ideas about women's rights and status that the U.S. has. Women have a subservient status in Moslem countries in general, but in Shiite countries, such as Iraq, their status is very low. Depending on caste, women in India have a much lower status compared to men. The same is true of many oriental countries.

The point is that if you marry a man from one of these cultures, he will expect you to act like the women he has grown up with. His family may expect you to defer always to his wishes, perhaps to live in a compound surrounded by the rest of the family, wear traditional clothing, and practice their faith. If things don't work out and you divorce, they may assume that the children belong to the father and will support him in moving them to their country. This is not fiction, it is happening every day.

Men who marry women from countries in which the status and expectations of the culture are very different may find some surprises, too. Some of the women who marry American men do so simply to gain American citizenship and escape the culture from which they came. They may then expect to be non-working wives and expect that their husband will be rich and take care of all financial affairs. Or they may be the sort who want to escape their past so much that they will tend to be very independent and not at all what you were expecting. If the relationship was built on the need to escape, the next thing they may want to escape from is you.

So look this all over very carefully. Do you really want to assume the values of another culture, and conform to their ideas? Have you lived in that culture for at least six months and experienced a realistic view of that society? You really should not make such a decision unless you have done so. If you don't want to live there, will you live in the U.S., and will he or she be content to live far from family and traditions? Do you know enough about how your intended's family lives and thinks to be sure that you want to be part of their ways of doing things?

Family and culture are powerful forces, as is religion. If you want to cross these lines, be prepared for some very difficult adjustments. There may be someone else with whom you can discover love without having to hurdle over all these barriers.

Chapter 12

And Some Really Practical Problems

The way of a fool is right in his own eyes, but a wise man listens to advice.

Proverbs 12:15

Sometimes, finding the person who will be the real love of your life boils down to dealing with some very practical issues, like career conflicts, where you want to live, friends, holidays, and annoying habits. Often these may mask deeper conflicts, but sometimes they can be the "little thing" that makes a relationship founder.

George and Ginger had married rather quickly following a three-year separation. They had known each other in college, but had let a long and fairly platonic relationship end as they had gone on to graduate schools at different ends of the country. George was a rather impulsive guy, and his seminary career was marked by lots of ups and downs, which we ironed out in late night debriefings after weekend fieldwork assignments. All of his friends were taken aback but not surprised when he suddenly announced that they were getting married after a brief two-week reunion. Ginger seemed like a rather fragile but lovely girl who was marrying something of a "bull in a china shop." We wondered if they really knew each other well enough to be jumping into marriage.

Their first Christmas came after a difficult fall in which they had to get used to living in a remote town in upstate New York. That, plus a rocky start with a difficult boss, and getting used to the long hours of separation that were part of the job, hadn't made for an easy start, but at least there was Christmas—their first Christmas to anticipate and plan. Ginger had always loved Christmas. It was one of the happiest times in her family when she was growing up. She set out to plan for it with all the fervor of a young bride in her first love nest. On a day when he was gone, she decided to put up the tree and decorate their apartment. She would surprise him with the wonderful sights, sounds, and smells of Christmas when he got home.

He was surprised all right. He was also completely upset. Why hadn't she asked him before doing such a thing? He didn't want to celebrate Christmas. He hated all the trappings and decorations and trimmings. He had good reasons. Every memory of Christmas he had as a child was extremely painful. Growing up with an alcoholic father, for whom Christmas was an excuse to get really drunk, and with a mother who was grimly determined to have an elaborate Christmas, no matter how miserable it was for the family, he hated every bit of the celebration. How dare she make him relive it?

It was a long December. And the thaw didn't ever really come. There were some other things they didn't know about each other that eventually drove them apart. But I think that first wedge in their relationship, when a girl who loved Christmas discovered that she'd married a man who hated it, was a very deep and painful one. Maybe it really was what drove them apart.

So, among the things you really should discuss as you are getting to know someone are how they feel about holidays, what they do to celebrate, and what things would they not like to continue as traditions in your family celebrations. You'll be surprised at what a gold mine of information those questions uncover. That is just the beginning of the practical topics we will cover in this chapter. Try these questions: *(Circle answers as applicable)*

1. What is your intended's favorite holiday? _____
   Don't know
   What is yours? _____

2. What family traditions about holidays would you like to make a part of your family? _____
   _____
   _____
   What family traditions would your intended like to make a part of your family celebration? _____
   _____
   _____

3. What family traditions would you not want to make a part of your celebrations?
   Yours:_____
   _____
   _____
   Intended's:_____
   _____
   _____

4. What is your intended's chosen career? _____
   Don't know   Doesn't have one   Don't know yet

5. What special demands does his or her career entail?_____
   _____
   _____

6. What is your chosen career? _____
   Don't know   Don't have one   Don't know yet

7.   What special demands does your career entail?_____
     _____
     _____
     Don't know   Haven't talked about it   None

8.   What bothers you about your intended's career or its
     demands?_____
     _____
     What bothers your intended about your career or its
     demands?_____
     _____
     _____

9.   How would you feel if your intended were more successful
     or made more money than you?
     Jealous   Like a failure   Wouldn't matter   Don't know

     How would he or she feel if you were more successful or
     made more money than they did?
     Jealous   Like a failure   Wouldn't matter   Don't Know

10. Does your intended really want you to have a career?
     Yes   No   Don't know
     Do you really want to have a career?
     Yes   No   Don't know

11. Which of your intended's friends do you really not
     like?_____
     _____
     Why?_____
     Which of your friends does he or she not like? _____
     _____
     Why?_____

12. Will your intended be willing to drop a friend that causes
     you discomfort?   Yes   No
     Will you?   Yes   No

13. Does your intended show any of the following symptoms:
Constant worry about weight (even though thin)?
Yes   No   Don't know
Excessive weight loss?   Yes   No   Don't know
Eating followed by vomiting?   Yes   No   Don't know
Eating followed by purging (using laxatives)?
Yes   No   Don't know
Compulsive exercising?   Yes   No   Don't know
Weight loss and skin problems, other health problems?
Yes   No   Don't know
Overuse of diet pills?   Yes   No   Don't know
Excessive weight gain?   Yes   No   Don't know
Compulsive overeating?   Yes   No   Don't know
Yo-yo dieting, usually not successful?
Yes   No   Don't know

14. Does your intended snore when sleeping?
Yes   No   Don't know
Do you?   Yes   No   Don't know

15. Does he or she have any other really annoying habits?
Yes   No

16. Is your intended reckless, do they drive dangerously, take
unnecessary risks, like to take part in dangerous sports like
bungee jumping, bull riding, etc.?   Yes   No

17. Does your intended have extreme opinions or prejudices
with which you strongly disagree and which may become
hard to live with in the long run?   Yes   No

18. Does your intended have to be busy all the time? Do they
become bored easily if they are not doing something with
other people or something entertaining?   Yes   No

Comments

Question 1, 2 and 3. Question 1 is a good way of tactfully asking your intended to give you a lot of family history. Be sure to ask them why it is their favorite holiday and what they like best about the way their family celebrated it. That should lead rather naturally into a discussion of what traditions you and he or she want to carry into your own celebrations. Listen carefully for clues about the way their family operated. If he or she is negative about the way holidays were celebrated, and has no wish to duplicate any of their family traditions, do a little probing. Was the family abusive, alcoholic, hypocritical about religion, or had relatives who were uncomfortable to be around or who were mentally ill?

If you discover some deep-rooted family conflicts or signs that your intended grew up in a dysfunctional family, now is the time to deal with the problems or decide that this is not the right person for you. If there was alcoholism or abuse in his or her family, have they received long-term counseling to help them undo the damage? If not, they should get help now before you decide to marry. If this is the first hint you have of real problems, go back and read some of the comments in Chapters 2, 8, and 9 about dysfunctional families, alcoholism, and violence. You have uncovered something of extreme importance to your future happiness.

If you learn that you have very different ideas about celebrating holidays, like that he wants to spend Christmas skiing, while you want to be home with the family, a tree, and all the trimmings, you can begin to see if practicing the fine art of compromise will work for you. If one of you is adamant that the only way to celebrate is the way you always did it, you are probably going to have problems discussing other issues that come up. Now would be a good time to get some help in learning how to communicate, before you carry unhealthy patterns into your marriage.

Perhaps you have discovered that you have very compatible ideas about family traditions and the kinds of things you want to have happen in your marriage. Great! It is these kinds of building blocks that make a good marriage even better. The more you talk about how you will celebrate holidays, how you will fit into or around family obligations, and what you like to do, the better off you will be when those challenges become part of your everyday life.

Comments on Careers

Many things in your marriage will be decided by your career or careers, yet often people enter into a marriage without really talking much about the demands of their careers or deciding if their career goals are really compatible. In the past, it was often assumed that the husband's career came first. Even if the wife worked, she was expected to make the move and change jobs if his career called for a move. Today, with more women having higher profiles and higher paying careers, the choices are more complicated.

Most career questions can be resolved if both of you are willing to do so, but remember that a person's work is a big part of who they are, how they feel about themselves, and where they spend a great deal of their time. If they are not happy in their chosen occupation because of a choice they have made because of you, or if you are not happy with some part of their job, your marriage could be in for big trouble.

Jim and Julie got married while both were working in the banking industry. In between having children and moving to take advantage of opportunities, both continued to work fairly steadily and advance in their careers. They didn't work for the same bank, and his career involved more sales work than hers did. It also involved the necessity of entertaining clients, something he very much enjoyed doing. Jim was gregarious and a good chef who enjoyed cooking up a large dinner or barbecue to feed clients. Julie was just the opposite. She preferred an evening alone to having company; she didn't enjoy entertaining or talking with clients the way Jim did. The only people she enjoyed being with were her family.

As the years wore on, other differences surfaced, but enter-taining clients became more important to Jim's career, and more resented by Julie. It became the focus of their arguments as she refused to help out and insisted that if he were to have clients over, he had to do all the work and preparation. She would often retire with a headache rather than play hostess. She would punish Jim by becoming more remote and spending her energies completely on the children.

That marriage ended in divorce. Career problems weren't the only reason, but they became major divisive issues that made other problems worse. Unstated expectations are like landmines in a marriage. Talk now about what you really want. If you want a career as a homemaker but are willing to work temporarily, now is the time to say so. If you want a career where you can leave it all at the office and not have responsibilities for entertaining, make that clear now. If your career is all-important to you, make sure your intended knows that.

Questions 4 through 7: These questions are starting points for your discussions if you have not had them yet. I realize that you may be still in school or have just started out in a job that may not be your real career choice. If that is the reason you marked "Don't Know" or "Don't Know Yet," fine. But you can still talk with each other about what kind of careers you want, what demands the jobs might have, and what you don't want in terms of work demands. If you say that you want to work no more than a forty-hour week, with weekends free, and that you want that for both of you, that is an important factor in determining the jobs you will consider. If you say you don't want to travel or you don't want your mate to spend a lot of time away from home, you are defining important career choices.

If you know the answers to what careers you will both pursue, what are the special demands that these jobs entail? Look espe-cially at demands like travel, specific job locations (such as if the job only exists somewhere you don't want to live, like Alaska or Saudi Arabia), frequency of moves, low pay, hours spent away from home, hours spent at home but still on the job, or on call. Some careers may have high expectations of the spouses even though they are not paid for the work they end up doing; for example, pastors of churches and politicians. Don't minimize the importance of these pressures. Doctors, police, and emergency personnel all have long and unpredictable hours. Military personnel may have long separations from family, as may oil drillers on offshore rigs, geologists for international oil exploration companies, merchant marine officers, and sailors. Even retail clerks and supervisory personnel in 24-hour business operations may be expected to work long hours or work evening and graveyard shifts.

Are you comfortable with the effect the demands of your career will have on your life as a family? If these extra expectations will interfere with having or raising children, what will you do? Will you decide not to have children and will your intended be happy with that decision? Will one of you drop or modify their career plans to take the major role in parenting? Will you both be happy if they do? These are really major questions that you will do well to agree upon ahead of time. Be sure that one of you is not telling the other what they think the other wants to hear. It is easy to think that you will cross these bridges when you get to them, but waiting to find out that your mate only said that he would stop work to raise the children when he had no intention of doing so will be disastrous.

Be realistic about the amount of loneliness you will want to handle. The wives of doctors and other emergency personnel who have to deal with long separations have significantly higher rates of divorce and alcoholism than people with less stressful schedules. It may seem romantic to be married to a doctor, a pilot, or a ship's captain, but do you want to endure day after day without seeing your husband or wife? And they aren't the only ones. I once spent time putting back together the marriage of a plumber who had decided to be on call 24 hours a day. I finally convinced him that it was permissible to use an answering machine during dinner and other important family times. No plumbing emergency was more important than his marriage!

Question 8: Pay attention to these answers. Some of the apprehensions you may have are negotiable; some are not. If you or your intended have some moral objection to the other's choice of career, such as that you don't want to be married to a bartender or the owner of a strip club, you should not get married if he or she doesn't want to change careers. Or perhaps you don't want to be married to a cop. You have no moral objection, but the thought of living in fear that he or she could be killed any time in the line of duty is enough to turn you off. Unless you can convince yourself otherwise by talking to other police spouses, you won't be happy being married to this person.

Any job that entails long separations, or that places one of you in constant contact with people of the opposite sex far from home, is bound to cause problems sooner or later. One of you will imagine something is going on, even if it isn't. One of the reasons entertainment figures have so many divorces is that they are trying to juggle conflicting schedules and long-distance relationships.

What do your careers mean to you? If you have a lot of your identity wrapped up in them, you will be less likely to compromise on the issues that your careers raise. That is, if you see yourself as a doctor and that means working long hours to you, you are not likely to think that you should change anything for the sake of your spouse or children. You will assume that they should adjust to your career. If both of you feel that way, there will be no room for finding a middle course.

To test the waters, try suggesting some workable compromise, such as changing shifts, or changing to a different department or location that would cut down the hours. If your intended wants to do that for the sake of your mutual happiness, you will probably be able to work out some feasible arrangement. But, if you get a string of reasons why it can't be done, or some other form of resistance, you may have discovered that he or she has a lot of ego tied up in the job.

If you feel that your intended does not understand the demands of your career, now is the time to make sure that they do. Ministers, doctors, police, military personnel, or fire fighters should especially make sure their intended spouses have a very good idea of what they are getting into. So should entertainers of any kind, airline pilots, long-distance truckers, and anyone whose career involves long separations or danger. Just because you enjoy what you do doesn't mean they will enjoy the consequences. And you won't enjoy it at all if they don't.

Question 9: This question may be hard for you both to answer theoretically, but try it anyway. In general, men have more problems handling what they perceive as a lack of success than women do. That is because men tend to value themselves by what they can do, and the yardstick of success is often money. They will feel less insecure about this if they are in a career they love that has its own intrinsic rewards, even though the pay is lower. Many men will feel very insecure if they are in the same career field as their wife and she outstrips him in terms of money or prestige.

So, this is a topic you really need to discuss. If you are both competitive people and you measure success by the amount of money you make, you can expect problems, especially if you are in the same career field. If at least one of you can say, "Look, I'm happy doing what I'm doing no matter what it pays, and I don't care how much either one of us makes as long as we are both happy doing what we like to do," you have found a winning formula for happiness and an emotionally mature mate.

One more issue to discuss is what will happen if one of you gets an opportunity to move in order to advance and the other cannot switch jobs in their career field easily. Just talking this one out now will give you an idea of how important each one of you thinks your career is. It will also tell you how well you can communicate about this very important decision.

Question 10: I suppose I could have asked this question first, but this is really a reality check that you should do now. I make the distinction between a job and a career. A job is something that you can leave anytime and pick back up if you need to. It does not have a career path that, if interrupted, causes you to lose upward progress. You can't drop out of teaching, corporate managerial positions, law, or medicine and drop back in at the same level a few years later.

Some husbands (this is more of a male problem) are comfortable with a wife having a job that they regard as temporary or at least subordinate to a career. They may really be hoping that their wife will quit working when children come along, stay at home, at least while the children are young, and then maybe go back to work to help kids through college. That, of course, is different from her having a career.

If that is what the wife wants, too, there will be no problem. But if you are a woman who wants a career, you will need to have a husband who wants you to have a career also. There will be a whole different set of priorities to manage, child raising will be challenging, and you will have to work out how you can both have careers that do not compete and which do not require moves that effect one another adversely. This can all be done, but you need to agree ahead of time that you both want careers.

There are men who don't want a career, and would rather live off their wives. These men are called gigolos, and you may meet one of them. Obviously, they don't make good husbands. As soon as they have taken all your money, they will be off to another, more attractive conquest. If you can't spot them any other way, they will be vague about what they do for a living, or pose as playboys, struggling artists, actors, or musicians trying to break in to the big time. If they need to borrow money from you temporarily to make a big deal, beware. You are about to be taken by one of the oldest con games in the world.

The female version of this type is the gold digger. If someone is more interested in your money than you, or wants you because they think you can advance them in their career, they are not the one you are seeking.

There are also men who may have the kind of job that is really not a career and who might really want to take over the child care and household management when that becomes necessary. They are rare, true, but you might consider marrying such a man if you want a career and don't care that he doesn't. But be discerning, make sure they mean what they are saying, and that they are emotionally mature.

Questions 11 and 12: Friends can become a source of major conflict in a marriage if you let them. It may be comforting to know that most couples' circle of friends changes after they are married. You won't necessarily be around the same people that you knew in high school or college unless you stay in the small town where you grew up. Even then, interests change, people move away or get preoccupied raising children or managing careers. So you probably are not stuck with his or her friends forever if they are people you really don't like.

People collect friends for a variety of reasons. Some are just neighborhood kids they grew up with. They might have already outgrown them, but they are not the sort they drop until they move away or take really different paths in college or careers. Others may be roommates at school, acquaintances at work, or people who may be involved in some short-term intensive experience (like a training class, retreat experience, or Armed Forces stint). Many of these may not continue to be long-term friends after the experience is over, but some may. Most will not cause problems for you, but some may. It all depends on how healthy the friendship was and what their reaction to you is like (and yours to them).

How do you define a good friend? Is it someone who you've known a long time, who you hang out with when you need something to do? Or is it someone who does certain things, like listen, help you when you need help, share your interests, or build you up? Do they know enough not to do certain things, like use you, talk about you behind your back, get you in trouble, take your things without asking? A good friend cares about you, sticks by you, and values your friendship. They are positive people who build other people up.

A bad kind of friend is just the opposite. Bad friends look out for number one and do not care who gets hurt by what they do or what they involve you in. They dare you to be as bad as they are. They may be the life of the party, but they'll make fun of you, and their jokes are always at someone else's expense. A bad friend tears you down to their level, or below. They monopolize your time, presume on the relationship, treat your things as theirs without asking, and value your friendship as long as you take care of their needs.

Obviously, good friends are good for a marriage; bad friends are not. Everyone probably can remember having a friend who turned out not to be a good one. Sometimes they are hard to shake; they may have a very neurotic need to have you as a friend, and they may have a hard time hearing that you don't want to be their friend any more. But the only constructive thing you can do is end such a friendship. It is bad for both of you to continue it, and it can hurt your future happiness.

So this question of whether your intended has some friends that you really dislike is really important. If they do, try to pinpoint why you feel the way you do about them. Is it because they have bad habits, try to monopolize your intended's time, don't like you (why?), are rude or otherwise socially embarrassing? If any of these are true, you may have good reasons for not wanting them around. You may also want to ask why your intended wants to have them as friends. If they are a bad influence on him or her, are they really to blame, or are they an excuse he or she uses for getting drunk or getting into trouble? This is a subtle but important distinction.

The old adage "birds of a feather flock together" contains truth. If many of your intended's friends are losers, heavy drinkers, promiscuous, or otherwise morally objectionable, what makes you think that they are not like them? If he or she associates with such people now, will they want to do so in the future? Do they enjoy doing the things the friends do? You are getting a glimpse of their character here, and you need to pay attention to the signs.

It may be that your intended wants to get away from such people, and you are providing the motivation for doing so. If that is what they say, make sure that they mean it. Set up a trial period during which they agree to stop seeing those friends. Observe carefully. What they do is far more important than what they say. Realistically, are they going to have to move away from these people in order to break the ties, and are you both willing to do so?

If there is gang or drug involvement, be especially wary. Do not overestimate your ability to reform your mate, or your ability to rescue them. Unless they have had some genuine religious conversion, or some experience coupled with counseling that really makes them want to get way from their old ties, don't assume that they will be able to do so.

If they have only one or two friends that you find objectionable, and you do not feel that your intended is so heavily committed to the friendship that he or she will not put you first, proceed with caution. If you think that the friendship will probably drop off naturally after the marriage, there is no point in making an issue of it now. If the person makes you really uncomfortable when they are around, however, you should let your intended know that, saying, "When Jerry is around I really feel uncomfortable with the way he treats other people," (or whatever specific behavior you can identify).

Notice you are not attacking your intended for their choice of friends, you are saying what you feel. This allows him or her to let you know how they feel about their friend's behavior, and maybe even suggest themselves that they don't see Jerry as much. Of course if they say that Jerry is their best friend and you'll just have to get used to him being around a lot, you have a clear indication of where you stand. You will need to think this reply over carefully before you continue the relationship.

Remember, if you ask your intended to give up a friend that he or she has known longer than they have known you, you are asking something special. So if you have a friend that he or she does not like, you can offer to make a trade. You can agree to drop your friend if he or she will drop theirs, or you can agree that you will see your friends separately but not involve each other in the relationship. This kind of compromise can work if the friendship is not a destructive one. If it is one you feel is bad, be willing to drop yours if he or she will drop theirs.

One kind of friendship that really should not survive following a marriage is a friendship with a former boyfriend or girl-friend. Old flames have a hard time not thinking you should have married them. They provide a fantasy that it is well not to nurture; sometimes they even meddle in your relationship. You should both agree that you will not keep up any of these friendships. One other kind of friendship that should not be allowed is that of a friend who wants to lure you back into the single lifestyle after you are married. If they want to take you or your intended pub crawling or partying by yourself after you are married, they are not doing your marriage any good, and are placing you or your mate in a position of temptation.

Question 13: Anorexia, Bulimia, and other eating disorders can and do kill people. Women are most susceptible to these disorders, but occasionally men will become compulsive about exercising and eating to the point that they damage themselves. All of these are treatable illnesses, but the person who has them is often so deep in denial that they will not accept help until it is too late. I have given you some questions to help screen for these disorders but your observations will have to be keen, for the victims are often very good at hiding their behavior.

The first symptoms are most observable. If your intended seems to be constantly worrying about their weight, even though they seem to be thin or even excessively thin, you may be seeing anorexia or bulimia. If they seem to have lost a lot of weight at once but seem to think they need to lose more, this is a strong sign. If you find that they are eating but vomiting or using laxatives to purge their systems of food, they need immediate help. They need to be confronted and taken to a doctor who deals with such disorders. You can find listings for physicians and clinics that treat eating disorders in the telephone directory. I will list some other help in Appendix B.

Compulsive exercising with the objective of losing weight is another symptom of anorexia or bulimia. Some people do become addicted to exercise not because it keeps them thin, but because it builds them up to look stronger. But those who constantly exercise to lose the pounds they need to model or do gymnastics and then keep going beyond the point of actual need are usually not eating properly either. If they become excessively thin, and you observe skin or other health problems, they are in an advanced stage of the disease and need help right away. Overuse of diet pills may add the complication of addiction to the list of things that need to be treated, and some can be very dangerous, causing heart and circulatory problems.

All of which adds up to the fact that if your intended has these symptoms, their top priority needs to be getting treatment before you do anything else about your relationship. Like other addictions, these may require long-term treatment and counseling to overcome. But unlike drug addiction or alcoholism, the person is less likely to relapse and the cure rate is higher. You will have to decide whether you want to stand by and wait for your intended to get the help they need. If you want to help, the best thing you can do is to encourage them to continue in treatment until they are really pronounced healthy and have had sufficient time to prove they can resist the temptation to fall into the old patterns. Doctors can advise you on how much or little contact you should have during treatment. You will really want to rescue the person, or badger them about eating, but they are the one with the problem and they are the only one who can fight through to a cure.

Another type of eating disorder is compulsive overeating. This may take the form of binge eating; yo-yo dieting, in which the person is always trying and failing to lose weight on the latest diet; or it may be a constant pattern of just eating more than a normal amount of food, plus snacking. Both men and women can suffer from this compulsion. In women, it often accompanies a history of childhood sexual abuse. The child adopts a strategy of being over-weight and unattractive to protect her from further abuse.

In other cases, food can become such a comfort in the face of stress that people become addicted to eating. Usually there is some kind of self-esteem problem at the root of such compulsions, so it is necessary for the person to discover why they are overeating before they can be helped to lose weight. Please note, I am not talking about a little bit of extra weight, nor do I think everyone can or should look like those rail-thin models. Compulsive overeating results in severe obesity, fifty or more pounds over normal, which can cause heart attacks and stroke. Comedian John Candy was a victim, as was comedian Chris Farley. Farley combined drug and alcohol abuse with overeating to end his life. Obviously, they were very unhappy people underneath their humorous exteriors.

If your intended shows signs of this kind of compulsive eating, try to get them to obtain psychological help. They may be deep in denial, and they may resist treatment. A videotape of their overeating that shows how bad they look might shock them into getting help. A confrontation assisted by family and friends may work better. As with other addictions, you can't cure them, but you can intervene and support them in getting the help they need. You can say, "Look, I love you, but I'm not going to stand by and watch you kill yourself. If you don't get help, I'm out of here." If that doesn't work, you need to realize that life with this person is liable to be short, if not impossible.

Question 14: I threw this question in here not because it is grounds for ending a relationship, but because I feel that anyone who marries a snorer ought to at least be forewarned. I have known couples who for fifty years have put up with trying to sleep to the accompaniment of sounds akin to train whistles, jackhammers, and buzz saws, but I've never known anyone who didn't wish for a cure. Fortunately, there are some modern day cures. The strips similar to the ones athletes wear to improve breathing seem to work well in alleviating snoring. There are other methods that help different types of snoring, including surgery. If you snore, you owe it to your future happiness to do something about it. If your intended snores, he or she owes that to you. Otherwise, separate bedrooms are in the offing, and that really cuts down on the romance in your marriage!

Question 15: If you came up with a list of your intended's annoying habits, the first thing to ask is just how annoying they are? Will they impair your future happiness together, or can you live with them? Nearly every wife has had to train her husband not to leave the toilet seat up, or throw socks on the floor, and you will discover a few more such habits after you are married. Inevitably, one of you will squeeze the toothpaste neatly from the bottom of the tube while the other will mash it from the middle. But are there things you know now that grate like fingernails screeching across a blackboard?

If so, now is the time to talk about them. You need to be diplomatic, and practice the "I feel" formula when talking about personal habits. You can say, "You know I love you, but when you clean your fingernails at the dinner table, it makes me feel like I'm going to throw up." Be prepared, he or she may reply with one of your habits that annoy them. In fact you might want to anticipate that by prefacing your statement with, "I probably have some habit that annoys you, and I hope you will tell me if I do." Then talk about their habit that bothers you. You may get a chance to stop habits before you marry that could drive you crazy later. This requires adult communication. If you encounter a huge reaction to a tactful approach like this, you need to reevaluate how emotionally mature your intended really is, and how anxious you are to live with someone who is so defensive that you can't talk about important issues.

Question 16: Reckless behavior is sometimes a sign of emotional immaturity, sometimes a personality disorder, and sometimes simply part of someone's personality. Sometimes the beholder defines it. A professional race car driver may be thought by some people to be reckless, but most of them are very careful about putting themselves in danger, and go to great lengths to make their cars as safe as possible. In fact, the reckless ones don't last.

Reckless behavior means taking unnecessary chances, endangering oneself or others for no good reason, and showing off by doing something dangerous in order to prove that one is braver or tougher than someone else is. This is immaturity, for the most part, though it can be a form of suicidal behavior. The problem is that this daredevil streak can be attractive, especially to women. It can seem to be part of a fun-loving, devil-may-care personality, but if he or she endangers you, they are not exhibiting loving behavior.

The question for you is how well that recklessness will wear over the long run. It may be fun while you are dating, but will your intended settle down when you are married and have children? If it is really a part of their personality, your marriage could be brief, and your insurance had better be paid up. Either your intended needs to do some more growing up, or they need help. Don't marry unless they do.

Question 17: Everyone has prejudices, and most are harmless. I may like Chevrolets better than Fords for no better reason than that my father did. That kind of bias does no harm. But prejudice against people of different races, classes, national origin, sex, or religion can do a lot of harm. Besides that, prejudice is not fun to live with. There is nothing less enjoyable than listening to someone who is constantly running other people down, especially if they are using foul language, dirty jokes, or racial slurs. Even if we share some of their biases, it gets old really fast. And to be married to someone whose conversation is demeaning to others becomes more embarrassing the longer one has to live with it.

Do you want to live with extremism or prejudice? Unless you have some very good reason to think that your intended will change, you should assume they won't. Prejudices are hard to change, and you will not be able to change them by yourself. They are only reversed by a life-altering experience or religious conversion. Unless you want to convert to their extreme ideas, be prepared for a long and unpleasant life.

Question 18: Does your intended have to be busy all the time? Are they easily bored? If you answered yes to this question, realize that this may be a sign of several serious problems. They may be simply spoiled. That is, they grew up having everything they needed provided for them on demand. That kind of treatment leads to an expectation of immediate gratification. It also leads to a very low tolerance of anything that isn't immediately fun or different. If life isn't fair they pout or whine. And it also leads to the need to be busy and entertained. But the need to be busy may also be a symptom of codependency, childhood abuse or trauma, or one of several personality disorders that are characterized by this compulsion to work or play too hard.

Please note that people have different energy levels, and some seem to be doing so much that they may leave us breathless after just talking to them. They may be operating completely normally for them, and this is different from a compulsion to be busy. Normally active people are not immediately bored if they are not doing something. They can relax, have a quiet conversation, or read a book without feeling like they have to be doing something else. People with compulsions cannot do this.

The warning signs of some real problems are busyness that seems controlling; that is, where every minute must be planned, where your time is controlled as well as his or hers, and where who you see and how long you see them seems to be determined by some schedule that may or may not make sense. When you feel that you are being controlled, heed that feeling. It means that someone else has a real need to be in control, either because they feel out of control themselves or because they have a need to manipulate you. This neurotic need may come from many sources, but it is a very unhealthy sign.

Do a little digging into your intended's family background. You may find alcohol or drug abuse, overly critical parenting, mental or physical abuse, sexual abuse, or violence. The person themselves may be a recovered alcoholic or drug abuser who is substituting this compulsion for the old one. This compulsion can lead to many behaviors that are hard to live with in a marriage. They range from perfectionism in everything from housecleaning to car maintenance and back, to workaholism, to rigid control of all family time and contacts, and to verbal and physical abuse of those (including you) who don't measure up to their arbitrary standards.

While this form of personality disorder is treatable, it is not easy to get someone to seek treatment because it is so easy to deny that it is a problem. It is easy to justify being busy. It can be ratio-nalized as being industrious, self-starting, high achieving, and all those other success-driven qualities that look so good on resumes. If you are not that driven, you will soon be labeled a slacker, lazy, not ambitious, etc. So if you find that your intended is compulsive and controlling, the best thing to do is get out of the relationship now before you end up in a marriage that will become sheer hell later on.

Do I exaggerate? Take the case of Monica and Harry. After a whirlwind romance in college, Harry and Monica married between his junior and senior year. Monica dropped out after her second year to help him get through his engineering degree, and he got a good job with a seemingly bright future. She had been impressed with his good looks, intelligence, and his drive to succeed. They worked hard, built their own little dream house mostly by them-selves, and had a beautiful baby girl followed precisely at three-year intervals by two handsome boys. From the outside, they looked like the all-American family. The children were achievers, not only in school but also in Boy Scouts, 4-H, and music at school and church.

But there was a dark side to this family. Harry was what used to be called a domestic tyrant. He worked very hard at his job but never seemed to catch a break. Even though the company broke promises, and went through reorganizations that cost him pension benefits and promotions, he stuck by them and worked himself to exhaustion when he could have moved to a better company. His anger at his slow progress at work was taken out in a relentless perfectionism at home. Meals had to be on time; homework, music lessons, Scout projects, and yard work had to be done to perfection and right on schedule.

Not incidentally, he would not attend church with the family because there were too many hypocrites there and he was too good a Christian to put up with that! Early on, Monica learned that he had ways of punishing her for any infraction. When one of the children, who was three months old at the time, cried in public on a vacation, he told Monica that he would never take her on a vacation again. He often traveled on his job and included stops to see relatives, but he kept his promise for thirty years. She didn't travel.

There was no relaxation whenever he was home. Since he was working hard they should all be working too. Above all, his daughter was to marry the handsome prince, and his boys were to be scholastic stars and successes at everything they did. Monica dispensed a sugary love and attempted to keep up the facade of the loving family that everyone thought they were. Emotionally, she bore the brunt of his tyranny by occasionally becoming physically ill and acting helpless. Like many victims of abusive relationships, she could not seem to do anything constructive to end the oppression.

I'd love to tell you this story ended happily, but it is one of those stories that doesn't seem to end. When his children disappointed him, he disowned his daughter for not marrying the person he wanted. They live as far away from home as they could get. His son, learning from her experience, tried to become a carbon copy of his father, but moved a long way away and has only been marginally successful in his career. The third son, having been told in every conceivable way that he was a failure, became emotionally ill. As far as I know, Monica and Harry are still married, but you could hardly say happily.

This chapter has been about seemingly small issues that can become very big challenges to having a good marriage. Dealing with them directly before you get married can help with some issues, while other issues are clear indicators that you should end the relationship now. Since I have suggested that necessity throughout this book, let's move on to just how you do that in the next chapter.

Chapter 13

Fifty Ways to Leave Your Lover

Blessed be the Lord who has not given us as prey to their teeth! We have escaped as a bird from the snare of the fowler; the snare is broken and we have escaped!

Psalm 124:6–7

Throughout this book, I have suggested that there are a number of clues that should tell you to get out of a relationship rather than get more involved. Fine, but how do you do it? And how do you get out without inviting further problems?

The Paul Simon song, "Fifty Ways To Leave Your Lover," seemed to suggest that this is easy: "Just walk out the back, Jack, make a new plan, Stan, …no need to discuss much, just get yourself free." But more of us would agree with the song that said, "Breaking Up Is Hard To Do." So this chapter will be about getting out, gracefully if possible, firmly if necessary, but definitely, finally, out.

First let me review some of the situations that mean that you should definitely end the relationship. One is obvious. If you suspect that your intended mate is violent or mentally or verbally abusive, get out and do it quickly. The clues are nearly always that the person starts out being extremely affectionate and considerate (too good to be true) but rapidly becomes very controlling. He or she wants you with him or her all the time, and isolates you from other friends and even family (you arrive late to family events and leave early). They may dictate what you wear and where you go. They are usually very jealous, and get verbally abusive if they think you are flirting or even looking at anyone else but them. They may apologize abjectly afterward and say that they only did it because it drives them crazy to think of you with someone else (this is the same line they will use if they hit you). Do not believe them. Now is the time to get out. The longer you wait, the less likely you will be to ever get out until you are seriously injured or dead.

A second situation involves alcohol and/or drug abuse. If you discovered that you have an alcohol or drug problem, you should break off any serious relationship until you have received long-term help and have been sober for a year. The same is true if you have discovered that your intended has a problem. You will only add to his or her problem by staying in a dating or live-in relationship, because you will be the unwitting accomplice to their patterns of thought and behavior.

He or she will try to make you feel guilty for leaving them, but you can only really help them by getting out of their game and making it clear that they need to take responsibility for their own life and get help. You will be far more helpful by standing outside the situation than you could be if you remained in it. Drug problems tend to be worse than alcohol problems. Combined drug abuse and alcohol abuse is even harder to cure. In any case, you can't cure it. They have to want to get help, and they are more likely to want help if they know they will lose you if they don't.

A third set of situations involves basic disrespect for you as a person. If your intended lies to you, cheats on you, demeans you or your family, or mistreats you sexually, you are not going to be happy in a marriage together. You are dealing with personality traits that most probably will not change. Since respect is really the basis of a loving relationship, you cannot expect a person who does not respect you to ever love you, no matter how much you may think you love them. Get out while the getting is good.

A fourth set of situations involves personality disorders that you may have discovered. The most difficult to deal with, such as codependency, bipolar or manic-depressive disorders, acute depression, and sexual dysfunctions, mean you should not consider marrying this person unless and until they have received long-term help. You may not have realized that some of the questions were screening for these disorders, but if you discovered that your intended was moody, depressed, had wild mood swings, or chaotic behavior, or had strange ideas about sex, you were being warned against marrying someone who would be very difficult to live with, no matter how attractive they might seem otherwise. There are better choices out there, and you need to find someone who is healthy enough to really love you.

A fifth set of situations involves various incompatibilities in values, lifestyle, family relations, child-rearing ideas, money handling, careers, religion, or some other issue that is vital to you. If you have discovered some major item about which you can't compromise and that you feel would make your marriage unhappy, don't disregard those feelings or that information. You need to have similar values and ideas about key issues in order to make a marriage work. If these are also combined with personality problems, behavior problems, or questionable family backgrounds, figure that three strikes means you ought to be out of there.

Each situation may require a different approach to leaving. And the degree of difficulty will depend on several factors, such as how long you have been in the relationship, how deeply the feelings between you run, and how normal the reactions of the other person are. It will also depend on you and how well you can communicate in a difficult spot. Whether you break it off face to face, by letter, phone, in a confrontation assisted by friends or family, or vanish without a trace, will also depend on the situation and what you judge to be the safest and most effective way to leave.

Obviously the most difficult situation is when you are dealing with a violent or abusive person. While I have written this book primarily for those who are not married or in a live-in situation, there may be some of you who read this that are living in this hell. You should know by now that it doesn't get better, just worse. You need to get out now before you or your children are maimed or killed. I know you are afraid that if you do something about leaving you will cause them to hurt you more; but if you stay, something else will give them an excuse to beat you or degrade you. It is not your fault that he or she beats you, but it is your fault if you let them continue or let them hurt your children.

The most important thing for you to do is simply to get out. Do not threaten to leave or let him or her know you are leaving. Do not stop to pack, you can get a court order to retrieve belongings later. Take the first opportunity that comes normally to leave the house, such as shopping for groceries or taking the kids to school, and walk, drive, or take the bus to the nearest police station, or a place where you can make a phone call in safety.

Call a Women's or Men's crisis helpline. If you don't know how to reach it, the police or a church or hospital will. When they connect you with a shelter, tell them your situation and let them help you make the decisions you will need to make. The police will want you to press charges so that they can take further action, but make sure you are out of harm's way so that you do not have to confront him or her. The location of shelters is kept confidential, and someone will come to get you and your children to take you there.

Remember that your primary objective is to get to someplace safe and then take steps to force the abuser to get help or at least leave you alone. You may have to press charges against them, get restraining orders, file for divorce, or all three, but the main thing that will protect you and give you some leverage is to get somewhere they can't find you. From there, people who deal with this all the time can help you decide the best course of action. You will probably communicate with your spouse by letter or phone rather than directly.

No matter how frightening it may be to be on your own, no matter how much you will be tempted to get back into the relationship at the first sign of their remorse and willingness to get help, realize that the best thing you can do for both of you is to give this person a lot of time to see whether they can change. They need long-term therapy, anger management training, and a good dose of the pain that separation from you causes, to motivate them to deal realistically with their problem. The sad reality is that the cure rate is not high, most abusers will not really cooperate with the therapy unless forced to, and the majority will pronounce themselves cured before they are. They will try to get their spouse to move back so they can continue to abuse them. Seventy percent of abused spouses go back, usually too soon, and often with tragic results. Please don't be one of them.

If you are not married to or not living with an abuser, I hope that the process I just described reinforces your decision to get out now. That scenario, sooner or later, is what you will be in for if you marry a violent or abusive person. To be escaping in fear of your life from someone who was supposed to love you, to give up home and possessions and have to run away, is not something anyone in their right mind would willingly choose.

Your objective and your choices are somewhat different from someone who is married to an abuser. You have no legal ties to this person, and no moral obligation to see to it that he or she gets help. Out of compassion you may want to help the person, but you will want to do so in a way that does not allow them to manipulate your feelings and con you back into a relationship before getting long-term help. You need to ensure that you put physical and psychological distance between the two of you for your own safety. The kind of person who is manipulative and abusive is also the kind of person who may resort to stalking or harassment to try to get you back.

I would suggest that you write him or her a letter. It needs to be very unemotional and straight to the point. It should be typed, not handwritten, and say something like this:

Dear Jack:

Last night you hit me (or called me a slut or whatever he or she did). You apologized but told me it was my fault that you had become so angry. That was not really an apology, and it does not erase what you did.

Hitting (or verbal abuse) has no place in a loving relationship. I respect myself enough never to hurt someone else that way and I will not let you mistreat me again. Hitting (or abusing) me hurts two people. It hurts me and it hurts you because you know it is wrong. I won't let you hurt yourself by hurting me.

You need help to find out why you are out of control. Go to a counselor. You owe it to yourself to learn how to control your anger.

I do not want to see or talk to you again. I have taken pictures of the black eye you gave me, and I will show them to the police if you attempt to stalk or harass me in any way. Stalking is a very serious crime. I am telling you this for your own good as well as mine.

Please get help, but do not contact me.

Sincerely,

Lisa

This kind of communication is really the safest way to deal with an abusive person. I do not recommend dealing with them face to face or even on the phone, because it is far harder to resist their pitiful pleas for understanding and their promises that they will never do it again. They have a long litany of manipulations they can use on you, and they are much harder to deal with when you are face to face or hearing their voice.

Be prepared. If they send flowers, send them back. If they try to phone you, have someone else answer for a few days and screen calls. If they are abusive to anyone on the phone, keep a record of it. Keep a copy of the letter to show the police. It provides dates and information they will need to get a court order to prevent you from being harassed. At the first sign of stalking or harassment, go to the police and get them to help you. The abuser will be more likely to quit if you deal with the problem quickly and firmly. Stand firm, you will eventually be so glad you did.

Leaving an alcoholic or a drug abuser involves a different set of priorities and options. If you are married to one, your objective is to get them to get help, then get help for the marriage. You should use any tool you can to compel the person to seek help. You can stage a confrontation with family and friends, threaten divorce, and actually file papers and force a separation, but you should not leave your home, he or she should. The object of the separation is to give him or her time (and I mean plenty of time) to get sober, get treatment, and get their own life straight before they walk back into yours.

The primary mistake to avoid is letting them come back too soon, before they have been sober and in treatment long enough to deal with whatever caused them to drink in the first place. They will whine and plead and beg to come back, but don't give in. You will also need to get help during this time to undo the damage that living with an addict causes. Only after you have both undergone therapy should you attempt to deal with any marital problems that were not caused directly by drinking or drugs.

One word of caution here: If the person is violent when he or she is not drinking or taking drugs, you should treat them as an abusive person rather than an addict. You should get to safety before taking action to get them to treatment. If they get violent only when they are drinking, you can consider forcing them out and into rehabilitation, as described above. If the person threatens you or causes property damage, the police may help you to force the person into detoxification. Get them there, and then proceed with filing for divorce or separation to force them to get real treatment. The separation papers should prescribe that the person get treatment for addiction and be certified as clean and sober for at least six months following completion of treatment before being allowed to reenter your home.

If you are dating someone and discover that they have a drinking or drug problem, your options are more limited. You have no legal ties, you have no real obligation to "cure" them, and hopefully you realize that you can't. You cannot force them to seek treatment. You can only deprive them of the one thing they may want more than their bottle, and that is you. How much effort you want to make trying to help is up to you.

If you simply want to get out of the relationship, almost any way will work. But be sure to tell them it's over when they are sober. You can tell them "it's not you, it's me," if you are afraid of hurting their feelings. You can tell them almost anything, and about all that will happen is that they will use it as an excuse to get drunk. Be aware that if they tend to get mean or violent when they get drunk, you may be in for a nasty confrontation before you are through. You should get out of range if at all possible after dropping the bomb.

If you care a lot about the person, and harbor some hope that you might have a future together if they will get help, you need to handle leaving with firmness and finesse. What you are about to do is not easy. If you are good at handling emotionally charged situations face to face alone, you may do so, but it may really help to have a friend, counselor, or clergyman along to lend support. Whoever comes along will be more helpful if they have observed the person's behavior when drunk or drugged and are willing to help you confront them.

I would write out what you are going to say. You might want to write it as a letter (handwritten) that he or she can keep. If you don't want to confront him or her directly you can send it instead. It should say:

> Dear Jim,
>   Last night (or whenever) you were so drunk (or stoned) that you vomited all over the floor and me and passed out. You probably don't remember the other things you did (include them, listing the most

degrading details—you want to shock him). You were really out of control. It was obvious to me and to everyone there that you have a drinking problem.

[Note: it helps to have specific incidents to point out, but if you don't, and you discovered the problem as a result of the questions in Chapter 2, relate what you found, such as "You have to have a drink in the morning (or, You drink four drinks every night). That is considered problem-drinking by the Council on Alcohol Abuse."]

I care for you, but I would not consider being married to a person who has a drinking problem. When a person drinks (takes drugs) no one and nothing else is really as important as the next drink. I refuse to play second fiddle to a bottle (pills). You are very special to me and to a lot of people, and if you have any self-respect you will not become a slave to a bottle (pills). But the only person who can make that decision is you.

If you decide to get help, I will stand by you and support you in any way I can. But I don't want you to get help just for my sake. You have to want to get help because it is the right thing for you. It will probably take quite a bit of time to go through treatment and I probably won't see you much during that time, but if you get your life back, it will be worth it.

If you decide you don't need help, then I am letting you know that I am out of your life. I respect myself too much to let your problem ruin my life. I care about you too much to let you hurt yourself by hurting me.

Make the right decision. Get help. Here's the number to call (Alcoholics Anonymous or Narcotics Anonymous or a hotline).

Love,

Sue

One way to handle the confrontation would be to go to him or her, make sure he or she is sober or just starting to recover from a great hangover, tell them you have something for them to read, and hand them the letter. If he or she denies that things were that bad, it is good to have others there to confirm how bad it was. They may be able to add other incidents where he or she was out of control.

Don't let the conversation get into an argument. If he or she refuses to believe you or the others, get up, tell them that apparently they don't love you enough to believe you, remind them that it is their decision whether to get help, and that you are gone unless they do. Then walk out.

This is tough love, and it is tough to do, but it is the one thing you can do that has a chance of working. You'll have to stick to your guns. If he or she calls, ask them if they are calling from rehab. If not, you aren't interested in talking to them. If they call from rehab and want to get out, tell them to hang in there, they are obviously not ready to leave. When they get out of rehab, you might go to AA meetings with them, but you should not get back into a regular dating relationship until they have been clean and sober for a year. AA will reinforce this. Don't give in, and don't give up. You may come out on the other side with the person you really do want to marry. But even if you don't, you will have helped someone on the road to recovery.

Leaving someone who basically disrespects you is really much easier than the first two situations. The main challenge is to say you are leaving in a way that makes them believe that you mean it. You are not obligated to tell them why you are leaving, and they won't necessarily change anything if you do. You may only be inviting an argument or annoying phone calls if you do. This may be another case where a short letter saying that you don't feel comfortable about your relationship ("it's not you, it's me") and do not want to continue seeing him or her might work better than having a face-to-face confrontation. It allows the other person the dignity of dealing with the rejection in private. If they call, you can be unavailable, or simply ask what part of "No" they don't understand. Be firm and it will soon be over.

The fourth situation, leaving someone who has some kind of personality disorder, calls for a decision on your part. You are not obligated to try to help this person or to cure them. They may be deep in denial and not realize that they have a problem. Whether you want to tell them they have a problem is up to you. It may not do any good. But it might point them toward help. Again, a letter may work better than a face-to-face parting or a phone call. People with personality disorders may be very difficult to deal with on the phone. They may be very manipulative and argumentative in person or on the phone.

What you say depends on how willing you think they are to hear it. If you don't want to explain what is wrong, the tactful "it's not you, it's me" should let them down easily. Make sure you state it in such away that you are not giving them hope that if they "fix" something you will take them back.

If you do want to tell them what is wrong, be specific and as unemotional as possible in your explanation. Saying, "During the time we've gone out, your moods have changed so rapidly and wildly that I couldn't keep up with them," or "I noticed that you were eating a lot and then throwing up after meals," or "You seem to be angry at everyone a lot of the time," will pinpoint the behavior that should warn them they are out of control. Then add, "I don't think you will be happy in any relationship unless you get some help with this problem. Please see a counselor, a minister, or someone you trust." Then close the door firmly but gently on the relationship, saying, "I do care about you, but I can't continue dating you. It would not be good for either of us." If he or she calls, tell them you will talk to them when they have finished therapy.

Leaving a relationship because of basic incompatibilities is simpler yet. You only have to decide whether to tell them why. I would recommend telling them the truth. I would tell them, for instance, that you couldn't see yourself being happily married to someone whose career would be taking them away from home for long periods at a time. Telling them that you do not wish to convert to their religion, and that you know that if you don't their family will not be happy, is also not insulting if you blame the decision on you. Most people will take this sort of ending better than a personal rejection. Writing a note in which you can word your reasons carefully may work better than trying to do this in person.

Be aware that they could decide to change whatever it is that is the barrier between you. If they say they want to do something like changing careers, moving away from their family, converting to your faith, or radically changing their lifestyle, they may mean it right now, but they could end up resenting you for making them change later on. They could also say they would change but not mean it. If you end up discussing such changes with them, you should declare a moratorium on dating for six months to see if they really do want to change. Especially if the change involves a religious conversion or getting therapy to change behavior, you need to remove yourself from the situation enough so that they have time without pressure to decide if this change is really what they want to make. Of course, you can avoid any discussion by just not telling the person why you are leaving.

Well, I didn't give you fifty ways to leave your lover, but neither did the song. I hope this has been helpful to you, especially if you are feeling trapped, or have never had to end a serious relationship before. But now that you've ended it, where do you go from here?

Chapter 14

So Where Do I Discover My Real True Love?

There is no disguise which can hide love for long where it exists, or simulate it where it does not.

La Rochefoucauld, Maxims

So you have read this far and have discovered that you haven't found the right person yet. Do not despair. He or she is out there. But where? Well, there are probably as many answers to that as there are people. I was talking to a lady recently about how she had met her husband some fifty years ago. They met on a troop train on their way to their assignments in World War II. Amazingly, they kept in contact and married at the end of the war. So I suppose you can say that people can find each other anywhere. It depends on whether you are really looking, what kind of person you are looking for, and what kind of attitude you take into the process.

You may have gathered from some of the comments in earlier chapters that there are some places that are better than others for finding the right mate, and some places to avoid. Bars, especially singles bars, are not the best places, nor are parties where the main object is to do a lot of drinking or drug taking. It might be a good place to find out how a person really acts when drinking, but that may be the extent of its usefulness. An exception may be some of the country western places where there is line dancing, or any place where drinks may be served but aren't the main reason for being there. But in general, you may not find these places the best places to meet someone, though they may be fun to go to on a date.

John White, in his book, *Dating,* suggests that the best first date is not a formal date at all, but any opportunity to have a cup of coffee and sit down for a chat where you aren't having to impress each other and can just get acquainted. I think there is a lot of wisdom in that. You need to see a person in a relaxed state to help you decide whether to go out with them. You can learn lots about a person just watching them react to normal situations, too. And asking someone to go for a cup of coffee is a lot easier than figuring out a big date.

Some good places to meet people are on the job; at activities sponsored by your church, synagogue, or faith community; or at places where you do volunteer work. All of these places offer you a chance to see how a prospective mate acts around other people, what they believe, and what matters to them. You can find out if they are interesting to be around without jumping into a dating relationship. You can find out about them from others who work or socialize with them. Ski resorts, recreational areas, workout places, and clubs may also be good, but they are also places where people do go to cruise or pick up people for casual sex, so there is more risk of meeting someone really wrong for you. People are more anonymous at such places, and you may not get a real picture of how they act in more normal settings.

But if you can meet your true love almost anywhere, how do you go about it? First of all, define what you are looking for in the person you want to marry. I hope you have gained some clues from this book. If your description stops at tall, dark, and handsome; or short, blonde, and sexy; better go back and read it again. Looks need to be somewhere way down the list. By now I hope that your description might include: emotionally mature; good communicator; non-alcoholic; non-violent; respectful and respectable person with similar values about money, sex, and the raising of children; has parents who will not be a huge problem to live with; and whose previous attachments, religion, and culture will not be a problem to your happiness.

Make up your own list, but make sure that you define those things that really matter to you. You will be able to immediately cross a lot of nightmares off your list on the way to finding the prince or princess of your dreams. By doing this, you may also get some hints about where to start looking. If your faith is important to you, then your faith community is the place to begin. If finding someone who shares your interest in music or theater is important, get involved in an activity where you can meet similarly interested people. If you are interested in finding someone who communicates well, you are more likely to find him or her in a Toastmasters club than in a research lab.

The next step is to evaluate yourself, something that this book has also hopefully encouraged you to do. If you want to marry the right person for you, are you the kind of person they will want to marry? You don't have to be the sexiest, or most beautiful or handsome person to be the right one. You do have to be yourself, be emotionally mature, be secure in your own worth and values, and be ready and able to communicate your worth to someone who will like you for who you are.

You also have to be reasonably attractive. By that I simply mean that you make the best of your looks and dress in such a way that you look clean, neat, and wear things that look good on you, whether they are the latest fashion or not. You need to smile and walk and talk like you are comfortable with who you are. If you don't, you are putting up barriers for the other person to leap over in order to find that attractive person which is you. So do you need to do a little self-improvement? If you need to lose a little weight, get a haircut, change your deodorant, improve your wardrobe, or brush your teeth more often, do so.

But most of all you need to be interesting and interested. If you sit home waiting for the right person to come along, you had better be living in a glass house in the middle of the mall. If you want to meet people, you have to be where people are. Even if you feel shy, you can go with a friend, but go. Again, it helps if you are doing something you enjoy or that has meaning to it. Volunteer for Habitat for Humanity, help with the Red Cross blood drive, or find some project at work that needs doing. Join the choir or young adult group at your faith community. You will find people that interest you at something you both find interesting. And it gives you something to talk about to get past the awkwardness of meeting for the first time. All of these kinds of things will make you a more interesting person.

But the secret of getting to know the person who will be your real love is to be interested in them. Ask them questions about themselves, how they got interested in what they are doing, where they are from, or what their favorite food or time of the day is. You will find out a lot about them if you just listen well, and you won't have to do much talking yourself until it becomes comfortable.

You'll notice that I didn't suggest starting by telling them something. If you are busy trying to impress them, you will usually shut down the conversation pretty quickly. They will think you are bragging or phony. Remember that every person's favorite subject is himself or herself, and if you listen to them for awhile, they will respond by asking about you, unless they are some sort of egomaniac or very insecure.

Love, after all, is caring about another person as much or more than you care about yourself. It is putting another person first. If you show that kind of interest and caring as you get to know people, a lot of people will like you. And among them there is bound to be the right person for you.

Chapter 15

A Few Final Thoughts

A new commandment I give to you, that you love one another even as I have loved you...

Jesus, John 13:34

Throughout this book, I have been writing from a spiritual point of view of which you may or may not be aware. I have used words that to me have a special meaning. As we approach a new millennium, I can't assume that you necessarily know or share those understandings. I at least owe you an explanation of what some of these words mean. One of those words is love.

Love in our time has come to mean romantic love, or sex, or the emotional feeling one has for almost anything from pets to ice cream. When used in talking about dating and married or unmarried relationships, it has been used so broadly that it begins to lose all meaning. Too often, it has become a word of manipulation that means "If you love me you'll let me..." or "If you love me, I can do anything I want and you will have to forgive me," or even, "Love means never having to say you're sorry," which has to be the dumbest line ever said in a movie. Love that is based on sentiment can be used and twisted to justify almost anything. The girlfriend of a young man who was arrested for the thrill-killing of two people whom he didn't even know said, "Well, I loved him. He's not a bad person really, it's not like he killed a whole bunch of people, and I hope he doesn't get the death penalty." That kind of love is blind indeed.

But real love is more than a feeling. Naturally, there are and should be feelings involved, but love, theologically speaking, is an action that involves a decision. It is the decision to care, or rather to do the thing that means you care and want the best for yourself and the other person. In the Jewish tradition, the love of God for his people is illustrated in his rescue of the Israelites from the hand of the Egyptians and his continuing love for them, even when they disappointed God and disobeyed his Law. He kept seeking them in love even though it meant allowing them to experience the consequences of their actions. God always seeks the best for each person.

In the Christian faith, God's love is seen in the sacrifice of Jesus, through whom God saves his people by paying the penalty for their disobedience and redeems us at great cost so that we can love and be loved again. God loves us ultimately and unconditionally. In both traditions, love is costly and realistic, and we are expected to love others the same way. Even in other faiths there is some version of the Golden Rule, which is a rule of love: we are to treat others the way we would want others to treat us.

The problem is that we hear the part about costly love and forget the part about realism. While Jesus sacrificed himself on our behalf, he did it with his integrity intact. He was not a doormat. He willingly took abuse and death because that was the only way he could save us. But salvation was his job, not ours, and it was done once and for all time. If we try to save someone from the consequences of their actions, we are presuming to be God, and we are asking for trouble. Our love for someone may be sacrificial, but it should not be unrealistic. We must know what we can and cannot do. We can help people by loving them constructively but we cannot save or rescue them without doing harm to them and to ourselves.

Love thinks about the consequences and looks ahead. Love does the right thing for both people involved. The media often confuses us about sacrificial love. It labels as a hero someone who jumps into a river to save a drowning person only to end up drowning himself. But had he thrown a rope or used a branch or a boat, he might have saved himself and the swimmer. People who are drowning in problems surround us. Some of them are people we love. We want to help, but our faith does not demand that we should drown ourselves in the process. The sacrifice we make is to set aside our need to be heroic, our desire to save someone from a heart-rending problem, our emotional bondage to the other person in order to do whatever helps them the most. Love is smart enough to do the right thing for both of us.

Often this may mean doing something tough when we feel like doing something sentimental. It may mean saying no when we feel like saying yes. It especially means that in relationships we won't let someone else talk us into doing something that would be less than the best for both of us. We will not let someone abuse us mentally, verbally, physically, or sexually because it hurts them and it hurts us. We will not let someone lie, cheat, or show us disrespect for the same reason. We will not let them ruin our lives by becoming accomplices to their abuse of alcohol or drugs. If they need help, we will insist that they get it, even if we have to walk away from them so that they will feel enough pain to want to change. This is tough, realistic, smart, Christian (or religiously based) love.

This is the kind of love that makes relationships and especially marriages work. It is emotionally mature love. Love based only on feelings can invite us into all kinds of abusive or distorted relationships. It can trap us into remaining in relationships that are sick, paralyzing us into inaction because we don't want to lose the other person's "love." But real love doesn't fall into that trap. We won't mistake guilt feelings or fears for love. We will do what is right for both people involved, even if it hurts in the short run.

Love in a relationship should be a two-way street. The person you love should love you back. And it should be with the same kind of mature, caring love that you have for them. Anything less will produce an immature, selfish relationship in which you will end up playing games or using one another. Never marry someone who says they don't love you but might learn to love you. Never think that you have enough love for both of you. Never marry someone who says they love you but who demonstrates by their actions that they are selfish, uncaring, or have addicted personalities. If you are committed to them, they should be willing to be committed to you.

The best definition of love is still Saint Paul's: "Love is patient and kind; love is not jealous or boastful; it is not arrogant or rude. Love does not insist on its own way; it is not irritable or resentful; it does not rejoice at wrong, but rejoices in the right." There is nothing sentimental about that kind of love. If you can insert your intended's name in the place of the word love and it describes them, you have found a truly loving person. A newer translation ends Paul's definition by saying, "It [love] always protects, always trusts, always hopes, always perseveres. Love never fails."

Marriage is another word that has a special meaning. In every faith I know, marriage is treated as sacred. It is not just a meaningless ceremony or a piece of paper. It involves taking vows before God to love one another for life. It involves asking God into the partnership of a marriage as the one who helps the couple live up to the commitments they are making. And inviting God in is what makes living up to those vows actually possible. Without God, it is really just the two of you against the world, and the world is an increasingly unfriendly place for marriage. With God all things are possible, including putting two very different people together and enabling them to weather the storms that life inevitably sends.

Now I know that many people do not take the vows or the sacred nature of the relationship seriously. And as a pastor I have seen many marriages take place in which the ceremony took last place to the trimmings, trappings, and the reception. You aren't treating a marriage as sacred just because you have it in a church or temple. But if you do treat those vows as sacred, you are getting your marriage off on the right foot, and you will seek the help you need from God to make a marriage that works.

If I believe that marriage is sacred, what about divorce? Well, I have written this book in an attempt to help you avoid divorce. For the better job you do at finding a really right person to love, the less likely you are to end up in a divorce. But that is just the beginning of the story. The real work of marriage begins when the ceremony ends. Even the best-matched couples find that they have differences of opinion, different ways of doing things, and different ways of communicating that need to be worked out. Keeping the romance in your marriage and getting past the disagreements and difficulties of life together takes commitment and effort. Illness, children, economic reversals, and a host of other issues can derail your marriage if you let them. With prayer, patience, and help, most difficulties can be overcome, but what if you hit an impasse?

When you need help and both of you are willing to seek it, there is usually great hope that the problem can be resolved. But when one of you is unwilling, then the threat of divorce may be the only way to get the other person to seek help. It should never be done lightly or when you don't mean it. You should go to counseling first (by yourself) to make sure you are seeing things realistically. But if you are, then you must be willing to go all the way, file for separation, and physically separate if necessary to get your spouse to make the move toward getting help and reconciliation. This is a tough-love approach, and the best discussion of how it works and the psychology behind it is in Dr. James Dobson's book, *Love Must Be Tough*. This approach does work and has saved many marriages.

But sometimes marriages end. Abuse, infidelity, severe mental traumas, or real and deep differences sometimes make it impossible for one person to keep trying. If you have been through a divorce, you don't need me to tell you what hell is like. Nor do you want to go through another one. I believe God gives us second chances in life, and he forgives our part in failures if we ask him to. While divorce is to be avoided with all the love and effort we can muster, it takes two people who really work at it to make a marriage succeed. Don't wallow in the failure. Learn whatever lessons your past has to teach you and go on. God may indeed have someone better for you.

Finally, do I believe that there is only one perfect mate for you? No. I never used the word perfect, because there is no such person, and if he or she did exist they would not marry you unless you were perfect, too. We are all made up of a mixture of good qualities and imperfections. I have tried to give you some help in deciding if someone is right for you, or if they have some real behavioral, psychological, or addiction problems that would tell you that they are really wrong for you.

I do believe that God has someone special in mind for you, and that if you pray and seek God's guidance as you look, you will find that person in the right time and circumstances. But that means you have to rest the decision in God's hands and not push the decision in some direction because you are anxious to get married. Pay attention to the negative information you get as well as the positive. Pray for God's will, not just your own. Be discerning. God has given you a good mind for the task. Use it as well as your heart and you can find a marriage that works with a partner who will love you the way you love them.

Appendix A

Complete List of Questions

Chapter 1: How's Your Emotional IQ

If you are under 21, ask yourself these questions (if you are over 21 skip these and see below)BE HONEST!:

1. Why do you want to get married right now? List at least three reasons.

   a. _____
   _____

   b. _____
   _____

   c. _____
   _____

2. Have you both completed high school, and are you planning to go on for more education?

   What kind of financial resources do you have that will enable you to get that education? (Will parents help?)

3. What kind of financial resources do you have now that will enable you to live the way you would like to live?

Stop right here and go back to Chapter 1 and read the comments about your answers. You may not need to fill in the rest of the questionnaire.

If you are over 21, answer these questions:

1. Have you had at least one year of living on your own (paying your own bills, managing your own life and work) outside a school or college setting? _____

Has your prospective mate? _____
How well did each of you manage? _____

_____

2.   Who (or what) does he or she put first in their life? Second? Third? Who (or what) do you put first?
(Answer this as you see him/her and yourself; then ask him/her to answer.)

Your Answer about Mate	Your Mate's Answer	Your Own Values
God	God	God
Parents	Parents	Parents
Friends	Friends	Friends
You	You	Your mate
Self	Self	Self
Work	Work	Work
Play (hobbies, sports, etc.)	Play (hobbies, sports, etc.)	Play (hobbies, sports, etc.)
Money	Money	Money
Success	Success	Success

Are the differences significant? _____
(See comments.)

3.   How does he/she solve problems? (If answers vary depending on the person or situation involved, note who or what seems to make the difference.)
__ Directly, meets problems head on and solves them
__ Indirectly, gets around a problem rather than solving it directly
__ Avoidance, ignores problem and hopes it will go away
__ Manipulation, cons or scams their way out of a situation
__ Blusters, shouts or bullies their way out of problem
__ Drinks or takes drugs to forget the problem, or to make themselves feel better
__ Blames other people or circumstances for the problem

Do you like the way they solve problems?
Yes   No   Don't know

Does it fit well with the way you solve them?
Yes   No   Don't know

4.   Is he or she ever verbally abusive, especially toward you? (Do you feel put down or in the wrong around them? Does he or she say you're stupid, worthless, etc.? Do they always have to be right, even at your expense?)
__ Sometimes
__ Never
__ Always (or a lot)
__ Enough to make me uncomfortable

5.   How would you describe his or her personality? *(Check all that apply)*
__ Ambitious
__ Easy going, laid back
__ Control freak, always has to be in control of situations and you
__ Happy-go-lucky, never worries about anything
__ Intense, serious about everything
__ Comfortable to be around
__ Quiet, never talks much about themselves or feelings
__ Moody, lots of ups and downs
__ Predictable, steady
__ Sociable, gets along well with other people
__ Unpredictable, never know what they will be doing next
__ Jealous, gets very angry if he/she thinks you are flirting (when you're not)
__ Helpful, kind to others
__ Self-centered, puts his or her needs first
__ A rescuer, often leaps in to save a situation and gets in over their head to the point where you have to bail them out
__ Forgetful, absent-minded

__ Mature, dependable, responsible
__ Good sense of humor, can laugh at themselves
__ Immature, pouts or throws tantrums when they don't get their way
__ Irresponsible, changes jobs a lot, careless about things and promises
__ Cutting sense of humor, uses put downs or racial slurs, tells dirty jokes
__ Uncomfortable, sometimes you feel like you are walking on eggshells
__ Angry, violent, picks fights, pushes you around and blames it on you
Go back and circle any personality traits that you **don't** like or make you uncomfortable.
Will he or she be fun to live with?   Yes   No   Not sure

6.   How does he or she handle conflict or frustration?
__ Directly, deals with the person or situation and works for a resolution
__ Indirectly, may not confront a person directly, but works out a solution
__ Avoidance, never deals with the person or situation and hopes it will go away
__ Manipulation, uses you or others to get their way
__ Irresponsible, blames someone else for problem
__ Passive/aggressive, is sneaky, plots revenge
__ Gets angry, fights or bullies their way out
__ Drinks or takes drugs to forget the problem or to make themselves feel better

7.   How does he or she get along with other people? *(Check all that apply)*
__ A loner, doesn't like to be around others
__ Not a loner, but doesn't like crowds, gets along well in small groups
__ Is comfortable mostly with family (Theirs? Yours?)

__ Doesn't really get along with other people on the job
__ Gets along well with others in most settings
__ Gets along with other people on the job
__ Is the life of the party, likes to be in the center of things
__ Gets along well with others, people like and trust him or her

8. What is their basic mental attitude? *(Check all that apply)*
__ Positive, hopeful
__ Cheerful, optimistic
__ Moody, ups and downs
__ Healthy, feel like they are well most of the time
__ Stressed, tired, overwhelmed by life
__ Anxious, worried about everyone's feelings, the future, etc.
__ Driven, angry
__ Gloomy, depressed, sick a lot
__ Negative, pessimistic

9. Is he or she basically truthful? Yes No
Has he or she ever told you something you found out later wasn't true? Yes No
Was it important? Yes No
Does he or she exaggerate about achievements or abilities? Yes No
Does he or she exaggerate about how pretty or sexy they are? Yes No
Is he or she secretive about money, background, family? Yes No
Does he or she often have to explain away things? Yes No
Has he or she ever cheated on you? Yes No

10. Is life around him or her frequently chaotic? (Are they always changing plans at the last minute, trying to do too many things at a time, overdoing things, trying to please

even people who don't matter, or involving you in rescuing them from situations they have created?)   Yes   No

Chapter 2: Alcohol and Drugs
(circle or check answers that apply)
1.   Does he or she drink?   Take drugs?   Both?   Both at once?
     (If no to all, skip to Question 4 and 5)
     If yes, how much? 1–2 drinks a day   3–4   5 or more
     Until he/she gets drunk/stoned   Until he/she passes out

2.   How often does he or she drink and or take drugs?
     __ Only on weekends or social occasions
     __ Has a drink or two daily (wine with a meal)
     __ Often has more than two daily
     __ Parties a lot, tends to get drunk when he or she does
     __ Seems to always need to have a drink or something to feel high
     __ Drinks at home even when no one is around
     __ Goes on binges, a day or more at a time

3.   Why would he or she say they drink/take drugs?
     __ To be social, fit in with the crowd
     __ Makes them feel more relaxed, more able to shine socially
     __ Helps them to forget troubles
     __ Helps them to have a good time
     __ Makes life feel better when pressures get to them

4.   Is there alcoholism in his or her immediate family?
     Yes   No
     If so, do they talk about it?   Yes   No
     Has the drinker gotten help?   Yes   No
     Did your mate ever go to Alateen or Al-anon?   Yes   No
     Did they get other help?   Yes   No

5. Is your prospective mate a recovering alcoholic/drug addict? Yes No
   If yes, how long have they been sober ____?
   Are they in some kind of support or therapy? _____
   Did they quit therapy? _____
   Why?_____

6. How do they treat other people when they are drinking/taking drugs?
   __ Mellow out, withdraw, fall asleep
   __ Get boisterous, rowdy, embarrass you
   __ Get sullen or mean
   __ Get violent, paranoid, start fights

7. When he or she enjoys hobbies or activities, is it partly or mostly because they offer an excuse to drink or take drugs? (Is the tailgate party more important than the game?)
   Yes No Maybe

8. What excuses do they give for behaving badly, missing work, forgetting appointments, etc.? _____
   _____
   Does drinking or drug taking have something to do with it?
   Yes No

Chapter 3: Respect Is the Bottom Line

1. Does he or she treat you with respect? (Include how he or she makes you feel, in public, in private, around their friends, your friends) *(Circle answers)*
   Always Most of the time Sometimes Rarely Never

2. Does he or she respect your saying "No":
   About places you don't want to go? Yes No
   About things you don't want to do? Yes No
   About sex? Yes No

About seeing other people?   Yes   No

3.   Does he or she respect themselves? Does their respect for themselves show in the following areas:
     Appearance (do they care what they look like?)   Yes   No
     How they treat their body   Yes   No
     How they treat their own things   Yes   No
     Is their word good?   Yes   No
     Do they work hard and do their best?   Yes   No
     Are they reckless, a daredevil?   Yes   No

4.   Does he or she respect their parents? (Are they courteous to them or rude? Do they refer to them respectfully when they aren't there to hear?)   Yes   No   Don't know
     If he or she does not respect their parents, why not?
     If there are real resentments, have they been healed or are there still deep wounds?   Yes   No

5.   Does he or she treat the following with respect:
     Peers (equals)?   Yes   Sometimes   No
     Waiters, salespeople in stores, hired help?
     Yes   Sometimes   No
     People in authority, police, teachers, their boss?
     Yes   Sometimes   No
     Minorities?   Yes   Sometimes   No
     Older people?   Yes   Sometimes   No

6.   Does he or she respect other people's property (including yours)?   Yes   No

7.   Are there any times when you feel that he or she is unfair, unjust, treats people wrongly, or cuts corners to avoid taking responsibility or paying his or her fair share?
     Yes   No

Chapter 4: Money, Money, Money

1. How do *you* value money? What does it do for you? ***(Check all that apply)***
    __ Having money makes me feel good
    __ Having money makes me feel secure
    __ Spending money makes me feel good
    __ Spending money makes me feel important
    __ Saving money in the bank makes me feel in control
    __ Saving money on a purchase makes me feel good or smart
    __ Money is a necessity, but I don't need a lot to make me happy
    __ Having money is a way that I know I'm successful.
    __ I like to shop when money is no object
    __ Money isn't everything, but it is way ahead of whatever is in second place
    __ In order to have the things I want, I want to have a lot of money
    __ I want the best for my family, more than I had growing up
    __ I believe a penny saved is a penny earned
    __ A lot of times it doesn't pay to try to save, or shop around
    __ I think budgets are for losers
    __ I like to plan ahead for spending on things I need

2. How does your prospective mate value money? What does it do for them?
    __ Having money makes him or her feel good
    __ Having money makes him or her feel secure
    __ Spending money makes him or her feel good
    __ Spending money makes him or her feel important
    __ Saving money in the bank makes him or her feel in control
    __ Saving money on a purchase makes him or her feel good or smart
    __ Money is a necessity, but he or she doesn't need a lot to make them happy

__ Having money is a way that he or she knows they are successful.

__ He or she likes to shop when money is no object

__ Money isn't everything, but it is way ahead of whatever is in second place

__ In order to have the things he or she wants they want to have a lot of money

__ He or she says, "I want the best for my family, more than I had growing up."

__ He or she says, "A penny saved is a penny earned."

__ He or she says, "A lot of times it doesn't pay to try to save, or shop around."

__ He or she thinks, "Budgets are for losers."

__ He or she likes to plan ahead for spending on things they need

3. How much money would you say it would take for you to be living the way you want to live? _____ (per year)
    How much would your prospective mate say?
    _____ (per year)
    If that means both of you working, are you both willing to do so?   How long?

4. Describe you and your potential mate in the following terms: *(Circle all that apply)*

YOU	POTENTIAL MATE
Spender	Spender
Saver	Saver
Giver	Giver
Taker	Taker
Miser	Miser
Generous	Generous
Thrifty	Thrifty
Careless	Careless
Careful	Careful
Extremely Cautious	Extremely Cautious

5. Does he or she use money to buy affection, to get out of trouble, to substitute for thoughtfulness or love?
Yes   No   Maybe

6. If it came to choosing to spend money on something you want, or something he or she wants, who would he or she spend it on? _____
Who would you spend it on? _____

7. Has he or she had credit problems or other money problems?   Yes   No
Are they cleared up, or will you have to live with them?
Yes   No

8. Does he or she like to gamble?   Never   Rarely   Often   Regularly
If yes, does he or she risk large amounts?   Yes   No

9. Does he or she have an expensive hobby or sport they participate in regularly? _____
Would they be willing to give it up to make ends meet?
Yes   No

Chapter 5: Sex, Sex, Sex

1. Which of these statements describe your attitudes or values? *(Check all that apply)*
__ I like sex any time, anywhere, with anyone I can get it
__ I think sex belongs only in a marriage or a committed relationship
__ I like sex with people of the same sex as well as the opposite sex
__ I think marriage shouldn't mean you always have to be faithful
__ I don't think sex is too important in a marriage as long we're happy
__ I like to watch X-rated films or other people having sex

__ I think sex is something really private. I don't even like these questions

__ I think any kind of sex is OK as long as both people feel comfortable

__ I think sex is kind of dirty

__ Sex is good if I feel good when I'm done

__ Sex is good if we both feel fulfilled when we're done

__ I'm a virgin, I don't know much about sex

__ I'm pretty experienced, but I don't want my mate to be

__ My mate needs to be sexy

__ Sex is sinful; I try not to think about it too much

__ I think kindness and tenderness are more important than sex

__ Sometimes I wonder if I like people of my own sex better than the other

__ The best jokes are dirty jokes

__ If my mate likes to look at pornography, thats OK with me

__ I like to dress up as a person of the opposite sex

__ If my mate liked looking at pictures of children having sex it would bother me

__ If my mate liked to dress as a person of the opposite sex it would bother me

2.   Which of the following statements describe **your potential mate's** attitudes or values? *(Check all that apply)*

__ He or she likes sex any time, anywhere, with anyone they can get it

__ He or she thinks sex belongs only in a marriage or a committed relationship

__ He or she likes sex with people of the same sex as well as the opposite sex

__ He or she thinks marriage shouldn't mean you always have to be faithful

__ He or she doesn't think sex is too important in a marriage as long we're happy

__ He or she likes to watch X-rated films or other people having sex

__ He or she thinks sex is something really private, won't discuss it

__ He or she thinks any kind of sex is OK as long as both people feel comfortable

__ He or she thinks sex is kind of dirty

__ He or she feels that, "Sex is good if I feel good when I'm done."

__ He or she feels that, "Sex is good if we both feel fulfilled when we're done."

__ He or she is a virgin, doesn't know much about sex

__ He or she is pretty experienced, but doesn't want me to be

__ He or she needs me to be sexy if they are going to be interested

__ He or she says, "Sex is sinful, I try not to think about it too much."

__ He or she says, "I think kindness and tenderness are more important than sex."

__ He or she has had homosexual relationships

__ He or she thinks the best jokes are dirty jokes

__ He or she says, "If my mate likes to look at pornography thats OK with me."

__ He or she likes to dress up as a person of the opposite sex

__ If I liked looking at pictures of children having sex it would bother him or her

__ If I liked to dress up as a person of the opposite sex it would bother him or her

3.   Does he or she taunt you with stories about old flames or conquests? Never Often Sometimes

4.   Does he or she talk about sex easily? Yes No

5. Has he or she ever been sexually abused?   Yes   No
    If yes, have they had counseling and long-term help?
    Yes   No   Don't Know

6. What is his or her parents' marriage like? *(Check all that apply)*
    __ Happy
    __ Average, not happy or unhappy
    __ Unhappy
    __ Divorced
    __ Divorced and remarried, now happy
    __ Divorced and remarried more than once
    __ Father was unfaithful, resulting in divorce
    __ Father unfaithful, but marriage continues
    __ Mother unfaithful, resulting in divorce
    __ Mother unfaithful, marriage continues

7. Does he or she pressure you about having sex?   Yes   No
    Has he or she ever forced you to have sex when you didn't want to?   Yes   No

8. Does he or she practice safe sex (if sexually active)?
    Yes   No   Hasn't in past

Chapter 6: But What About the Children?

1. Do you want to have children?   Yes   No
    Why or why not?

    What does having a child or children mean to you?

2. Does he or she want to have children?   Yes   No
    Why or why not?

    What does having a child or children mean to him or her?

3. How many children would you like to have?
    How many would he or she like to have?

If your responses are different, what do you think he or she is really saying?

4. When do you want to have children?
   When does he or she want to have children?
   If your responses are different, are the two of you willing to compromise on this?

5. What do you see as the sacrifices necessary for raising children?

   What does he or she see as the sacrifices necessary for raising children?

6. What part do you expect your prospective mate to play in child raising and care?
   What part does he or she see themselves and you playing?

7. If your family were everything you wanted it to be, how would you describe it in a word or a phrase?
   How would he or she describe it?

8. Do you believe in spanking or mild corporal punishment as part of disciplining children?
   Does your prospective mate?

Chapter 7: Some Previous Attachments
(Circle answers that apply)
1. What is your marital status?
   Single, never married   Widowed   Divorced
   Divorced more than once
   Single, ended long-term relationship

   If formerly married, how long has it been since you ended that marriage or relationship? _____ Did you get counseling before or after the breakup? _____

2.   What is your prospective mate's marital status?
Single, never married   Widowed   Divorced
Divorced more than once
Single, ended long-term relationship

If formerly married, how long has it been since she or he ended that marriage or relationship? _____ Did they get counseling before or after the breakup? _____

3.   Are there still a lot of hard feelings and difficulties left over from the former relationship?
For You: Yes, on my part   No, on my part
Yes, on ex's part   No, on ex's part
For Mate: Yes, on their part   No, on their part
Yes, on ex's part   No, on ex's part
How difficult do you think these will be to deal with?

4.   Are there children? No *(Skip to comments or go to questions for Chap. 8)*
Yes; mine, ages _____
Yes; his or hers, ages _____

5.   Who has custody? Yours: _____   Prospective mate's ____
Have visitation rights, times, and places been clearly established?   Yes   No   Joint custody
Are you comfortable with the arrangements?   Yes   No
Don't know

6.   Have you met your prospective mate's children?   Yes   No
If yes, do you like them?   Yes   No
Do they like you?   Yes   No

Has he or she met your children?   Yes   No
If yes, does he or she like them?   Yes   No
Do they like him or her?   Yes   No

7. If there are grandparents on either side, have you and your prospective mate met them? Yes No
Are they willing to accept you and him or her as part of the family? Yes No

Chaptr 8: Violence
(Circle answers)

1. Does your prospective mate have a "hot temper?"
Yes No

2. Does he/she seem angry a lot of the time they are around you? Yes No

3. Has your prospective mate ever hit you? Yes No
Intentionally? Yes No

4. Has he or she hit anyone of opposite sex? Yes No
Intentionally? Yes No

5. Does he or she handle anger by throwing things?
Yes No
Hitting things? Yes No
Smashing things? Yes No

6. How does his or her family handle anger? Specifically, is there any pattern of violence between his or her parents?
Yes No
Between other family members? Yes No

7. Is there any history of abuse in his or her family?
Yes No
Was he or she abused physically or sexually? Yes No

8. Has he or she ever abused a cat, dog, or other pet?
Yes No

9.   Does he or she have a criminal record for violent behavior?
      Yes   No

Chapter 9: In-laws or Outlaws?
(Circle answers where applicable)

1.   Have you met your prospective mate's parents?   Yes   No
      (If No, and it is not possible to meet them before you marry,
      you should talk to your mate about them and attempt to
      answer as many of the rest of these questions as you can,
      based on the information he or she supplies.)

2.   Do you like them?   Yes   No   Not sure
      Do they make you feel welcome?   Yes   No   Not sure
      Do you feel comfortable around them?
      Yes   No   Not sure
      If No, why not? _____

3.   Do they like you?   Yes   No   Not sure
      How do they feel about you as a prospective mate for their
      son or daughter? _____
      _____

4.   How possessive are they about their son or daughter? Do
      they want him or her to be independent, or to be around
      them all of the time? Will they feel his or her first loyalty
      is to you or them? Do they control his or her job or
      fortune?

5.   Has your prospective mate met your parents?   Yes   No
      (If No, and it is not possible for them to meet before you
      marry, answer the next questions on your best estimate of
      their reactions. Do not be overly optimistic!)

6.   Does he or she like them?   Yes   No   Not sure
      Does he or she feel welcome?   Yes   No   Not sure
      Does he or she feel comfortable around them?

Yes   No   Not sure
If No, why not? _____

7. Do they like him or her?   Yes   No   Not sure
    How do they feel about him or her as a prospective mate for
    their son or daughter? _____
    _____

8. How possessive are they about you? Do they want you to be
    independent, or to be around *them* all of the time? Will they
    feel your first loyalty is to you or them? Do they control
    your job or fortune?

9. How well do you think your parents will get along with his
    or her parents?

10. How close will you be living to your in-laws and your
    parents? Will there be frequent contact?

11. Will you be living with either set of parents after you are
    married?

12. How important is it to your prospective mate to have good
    relations with your parents and his or hers?
    Very important   Somewhat important   Not important
    Whose responsibility will it be to maintain those relation-
    ships?

Chapter 10: Can We Talk?!?
(Circle answers)

1. Are you a better talker or a listener?
    Talker   Listener   Don't know
    Is your prospective mate a better talker or listener?
    Talker   Listener   Don't know
    (If either question results in a Don't know, ask your family
    or their friends)

2. Does your prospective mate avoid conflict at all costs when talking with you or others?   Yes   No   Some of the time   Most of the time   Almost always

3. How have you handled disagreements? *(Check all that apply)*
    __ One of us leaves in the middle of an argument
    __ One of us gets our way by crying or pouting
    __ One of us slams the door and walks out
    __ We never raise our voices
    __ One of us may leave the room to calm down but comes back and talks later
    __ We talk things through until we reach a conclusion
    __ We never have any disagreements
    __ One of us solves things by never admitting there is a problem
    __ One of us is always the one who gives in

4. Can you express your feelings to your potential mate without him/her becoming defensive?
    Yes   No   Sometimes   Rarely
    Can you express your feelings to your potential mate without becoming defensive yourself?
    Yes   No   Sometimes   Rarely

5. What do you talk about most of the time? *(Check any but circle the major ones)*

__ Work	__ Parties	__ Drinking
__ Sports	__ Clothes	__ Drugs
__ Other people	__ Future plans	__ School
__ Sex	__ Feelings	__ Likes/dislikes
__ Money	__ Children	

    __ Common hobbies, interests
    __ His/her interests or hobbies
    __ Other_____

6.   Is your prospective mate's talk mostly positive or negative?
      Positive   Negative

7.   Do you feel manipulated, controlled, or put down in your talk with him/her?
      Yes   No   Sometimes   Rarely   Often
      Do you feel like you can never win?
      Yes   No   Sometimes   Rarely   Often

Chapter 11: Religious and Cultural Differences

First, list your and your prospective mate's religious and ethnic information:

Religion, Denomination, Nationality/Ethnic group, Race

Yours_____

His\hers_____

[Note: *Religion* means major religious group: Christianity, Judaism, Buddhism, Islam, Hinduism, Jainism, Sikhism, Confucianism, Taoism, Shintoism, Zoroastrianism, or B'hai. *Denomination* means a branch of a religion, such as Roman Catholic, Presbyterian, or Baptist denominations of Christianity; Sunni or Shiite branches of Islam; or Nichiren or Zen branches of Buddhism. For the purpose of this questionnaire, list Jehovah's Witnesses, Mormonism, and Christian Science as denominations under Christianity. List New Age under Hinduism.]

(Circle answers where applicable)

1.   How important is your faith to you?
      Very important   Somewhat important   Unimportant

      How important is it to your prospective mate?
      Very important   Somewhat important   Unimportant

2.   Does he or she:
      Attend worship services?
      Regularly   Occasionally   Rarely   Never
      Take part in Church/religious activities?
      Regularly   Occasionally   Rarely   Never

Pray?
Regularly   Occasionally   Rarely   Never
Say prayers at meals?
Regularly   Occasionally   Rarely   Never
Talk about faith with you or others?
Regularly   Occasionally   Rarely   Never
Give money regularly?
Regularly   Occasionally   Rarely   Never
Read Scripture or religious literature?
Regularly   Occasionally   Rarely   Never

3. Do you:

Attend worship services?
Regularly   Occasionally   Rarely   Never
Take part in Church/religious activities?
Regularly   Occasionally   Rarely   Never
Pray?
Regularly   Occasionally   Rarely   Never
Say prayers at meals?
Regularly   Occasionally   Rarely   Never
Talk about faith with him/her or others?
Regularly   Occasionally   Rarely   Never
Give money regularly?
Regularly   Occasionally   Rarely   Never
Read Scripture or religious literature?
Regularly   Occasionally   Rarely   Never

4. Does his/her faith seem to influence their everyday behavior and ethics?
Yes   No   Somewhat   A Lot   Not sure
Does yours?
Yes   No   Somewhat   A Lot   Not sure

5. How important is it to your parents that you marry someone of the same faith or denomination?
Important   Somewhat important   Not at all

How important is it to his/her parents that they marry someone of the same faith or denomination?
Important   Somewhat important   Not at all

6. As a condition of getting married, will either of you have to convert to the other's religion or faith group?   Yes   No
If yes, how do you feel about that?
How does he/she feel?

7. If one of you is of another faith group, are there also national or cultural differences that are involved? (For example, your fiancé is a Moslem from Lebanon)
Yes   No
If yes, do you have a good idea of the expectations of a wife or husband in that culture?

Chapter 12: And Some Really Practical Problems

1. What is your intended's favorite holiday? _____
Don't know
What is yours? _____

2. What family traditions about holidays would you like to make a part of your family? _____
_____
What family traditions would your intended like to make a part of your family celebration? _____
_____

3. What family traditions would you not want to make a part of your celebrations?
Yours:_____
_____
_____
Intended's:_____
_____
_____

4. What is your intended's chosen career? _____
    Don't know   Doesn't have one   Don't know yet

5. What special demands does his or her career entail?_____
    _____
    _____

6. What is your chosen career? _____
    Don't know   Don't have one   Don't know yet

7. What special demands does your career entail?_____
    _____
    _____
    Don't know   Haven't talked about it   None

8. What bothers you about your intended's career or its
    demands?_____
    _____
    What bothers your intended about your career or its
    demands?_____
    _____
    _____

9. How would you feel if your intended were more successful
    or made more money than you?
    Jealous   Like a failure   Wouldn't matter   Don't know
    How would he or she feel if you were more successful or
    made more money than they did?
    Jealous   Like a failure   Wouldn't matter   Don't Know

10. Does your intended really want you to have a career?
    Yes   No   Don't know
    Do you really want to have a career?
    Yes   No   Don't know

11. Which of your intended's friends do you really not

like?_____

_____

Why?_____
Which of your friends does he or she not like? _____

_____

Why?_____

12. Will your intended be willing to drop a friend that causes you discomfort?   Yes   No
Will you?   Yes   No

13. Does your intended show any of the following symptoms:
Constant worry about weight (even though thin)?
Yes   No   Don't know
Excessive weight loss?   Yes   No   Don't know
Eating followed by vomiting?   Yes   No   Don't know
Eating followed by purging (using laxatives)?
Yes   No   Don't know
Compulsive exercising?   Yes   No   Don't know
Weight loss and skin problems, other health problems?
Yes   No   Don't know
Overuse of diet pills?   Yes   No   Don't know
Excessive weight gain?   Yes   No   Don't know
Compulsive overeating?   Yes   No   Don't know
Yo-yo dieting, usually not successful?
Yes   No   Don't know

14. Does your intended snore when sleeping?
Yes   No   Don't know
Do you?   Yes   No   Don't know

15. Does he or she have any other really annoying habits?
Yes   No

16. Is your intended reckless, do they drive dangerously, take unnecessary risks, like to take part in dangerous sports like bungee jumping, bull riding, etc.?   Yes   No

17.   Does your intended have extreme opinions or prejudices
       with which you strongly disagree and which may become
       hard to live with in the long run?   Yes   No

18.   Does your intended have to be busy all the time? Do they
       become bored easily if they are not doing something with
       other people or something entertaining?   Yes   No

Appendix B

Where to Get Help

Throughout the book, I have suggested that you or your intended may need to seek help in the case of various addictions or behavioral problems. In the case of addictions, group therapies of the kind pioneered by Alcoholics Anonymous tend to have the best track record for keeping people off of addictions. Many other groups have started using similar steps to help. Here is a listing of the major ones.

Alcoholics Anonymous (AA): To find out more about their Organization, write: AA, Box 459, Grand Central Station, New York, NY 10163, for video and literature. For local meetings and times, look under Alcoholics Anonymous in your local telephone directory. You can find more information online at http://www.aa.org.

Al-Anon: This is the support group for family and friends of alcoholics. It includes Alateen, which helps younger family members cope with drinking problems in their family. Al-Anon publishes The Forum, a monthly magazine ($10 per year). Write: Al-Anon, 1600 Corporate Landing Parkway, Virginia Beach, VA 23454-5617, or call: 757-563-1600. For local meeting information, call 1-888-4AL-ANON toll free. Or see their web page at http://www.al-anon.org. There is an online group called Key To Harmony, located at http://www.keytoharmony.org

Narcotics Anonymous (NA): This organization has free groups for recovering addicts to various drugs. NA publishes a newsletter, Meeting By Mail, as well as a monthly magazine, The NA Way, which is free. Literature and tapes are available by writing: NA, PO Box 9999, Van Nuys, CA 91409. Call (818) 773-9999, or fax (818) 700-0700. Or check out their very complete Web Page at http://www.na.org.

Gamblers Anonymous (GA): This organization assists compulsive gamblers in overcoming this addiction. GA publishes

Lifeline Bulletin for its membership at $25 per year. Other information is available by writing: GA, PO Box 17173, Los Angeles, CA 90017. Or call: (213) 386-8789, fax (213) 386-0030. They have a web page at http://www.gamblersanonymous.org.

Gam-Anon: Similar to Al-Anon, this is a twelve-step support group for the family and friends of compulsive gamblers. Lots of good literature and a quarterly newsletter are available by writing: Gam-Anon, PO Box 157, Whitestone, NY 11357. Or call: (718) 352-1671. There is a web page at http://www.gamblersanonymous.org.gamanon.html.

Debtors Anonymous (DA): This organization meets to help people who abuse credit, accept loans without proper collateral, or have other overspending problems. For information, write DA General Service Office, PO Box 888, Needham, MA 02492-0009, or call (781) 453-2743. They have a web page at http://www.debtorsanonymous.org.

Overeaters Anonymous (OA): This is for men and women seeking to recover from overeating, For their monthly magazine, Lifeline (12.99/year), or other literature write: OA, PO Box 44020, Rio Rancho, NM 87174-4020, or call (505) 891-2664. They have a web site at http://www.overeatersanonymous.org.

Food Addicts Anonymous (FAA): Provides assistance to food-addicted people. For information and quarterly newsletter called Abstinence Times ($12/year), write: FAA, 4623 Forrest Hill Blvd., Suite 109-4, West Palm Beach, FL 33415, or call: (561) 967-3871.

National Association of Anorexia Nervosa and Associated Disorders (ANAD): This is the oldest nonprofit organization in the U.S., which helps people recover from anorexia, bulimia, and binge eating. Support groups are available for people fighting these disorders as well as groups for their families and friends. For information write to: ANAD, Box 7, Highland Park, IL 60035, or call: (847) 831-3438. There are a number of other organizations and information sites on the web: use any search engine to search under Anorexia.

Codependents Anonymous: This organization assists in the

recovery of people caught in the trap of codependency, whether it is caused by growing up in an alcoholic family (ACOA) or other reasons. There is a wide range of support groups for people with differing problems, such as loving too much, anger management, etc. Their web site at http://www.ourcoda.org is a good source of information and lists local groups. Write for their main manual at: CoDA, PO Box 704, Vista, CA 92083-0704, or call (760) 730-0663. For other publications write: CoRe Publications, PO Box 670861, Dallas, TX 75367-0861. Send e-mail to core-publishing@usa.net.

Most of the organizations have local listings for groups in the telephone books of larger cities. All have worthwhile information, and some of the web sites actually list the local contact numbers. So if you need help quickly, you can usually get it. You can also get good information from any of the hotlines listed in your telephone directory.

Counseling and Counseling Services

There is a bewildering array of listings in the average large city telephone directory. Because there is no national system for certifying counselors, almost anyone can hang up a shingle as a counselor. They may or may not be competent, and their abilities will depend on their training. Here is some information that will help you sort them out. There are differences in title, which tell you something about their training and the kind of help they can offer.

Counselor is the broadest term. People with virtually no formal training can call themselves counselors, but people with Ph.D.'s will also list themselves as counselors. So you should look to see what other licenses and degrees they have. If they show LSW or LCSW behind the name, it means they are a Licensed (Clinical) Social Worker, under the licensing requirements of the State. LMFT means Licensed Marriage and Family Therapist. Licensing means that they have met at least some state requirements and are regulated in the way they conduct their operation. You can call the state licensing board to find out if they are currently licensed and if there have been complaints.

Look for the degrees behind the name: MSW means they have a master's degree in Social Work; M.Ed. is another recognized degree in professional counseling. A Ph.D. or Ed.D. shows that they have earned a doctorate in these fields. In general, unless a counselor has some advanced degree and is licensed, you are taking a chance in going to him or her.

Christian Counselor is another generic term. It can mean little or no training, training in applying scripture to problems, or professional training. In general, this term will indicate someone who is on a staff of a church to do counseling, but you will have to ask what their training is. There is a professional association for them called the American Association of Christian Counselors. Membership in this association may indicate more proficiency compared to those who are not members.

Pastoral Counselors are people who have an advanced degree from a theological seminary, plus a degree or considerable training in clinical pastoral counseling. Their degrees will be an M.Div., Th.M., Th.D., or D.Min., plus an MSW or other master's degree in counseling. They will usually be licensed and will belong to the American Association of Pastoral Counselors, which promotes training and continuing improvement of its membership. They may work on a church staff or with a counseling service. In general, these are very competent and well-trained professionals, capable of handling a wide range of problems and very careful to refer you if they are out of their depth.

Pastoral Psychotherapists are pastoral counselors who work in a clinical setting and have taken further training in various specialized therapies. They are trained, for instance, in regression therapy, which is necessary for treating victims of child abuse. These are well-trained and regulated counselors who handle severe and deep-rooted behavior problems. They will handle alcohol and drug problems after the person has gone through detoxification. They will belong to the American Association of Pastoral Counselors.

Psychologists have a degree in psychology and usually at least an MSW or other master's or doctoral degree. They will almost always be licensed, if they are legitimate. They deal well with the usual marriage, family, behavior, and learning problems. They tend to work in secular (non-religious) settings such as county mental health clinics or private practices. They will refer patients to psychotherapists or psychiatrists when problems are too severe or too long-term for them to deal with. They cannot dispense medication.

Psychotherapists generally have more training than psychologists and do long-term therapy for people with deeper problems. They may have doctorates and have completed clinical training in various forms of therapy. They may operate in private or public settings. They will be licensed, and will belong to the American Counseling Association or other professional psychological associations.

Psychiatrists are Medical Doctors with additional specialization in psychotherapy. They will have an M.D. in their credentials. They are licensed and allowed to dispense medication for patients who have disorders such as depression or bipolar disorders that certain drugs can help. They have gone through therapy themselves if they practice psychotherapy. They will usually be attached to some hospital, but may have a private practice as well. In other words, they are highly trained and will belong to professional associations.

Counseling Services range from secular clinics with one or more staff members to religious services. The religious services, such as Lutheran Family Services, Jewish Family Services, Catholic Services (names may vary), and Samaritan Counseling Centers generally have only accredited personnel on staff that range from counselors to pastoral psychotherapists. They will usually have a liaison with a psychiatrist to enable them to medicate those needing it. In general, they will be less expensive than private practice therapists and will often be able to assist with costs through special funds. One of the advantages of such services is that the therapists can consult each other regularly on difficult cases and help each other lay out the treatments that will be most likely to help.

Any legitimate counseling service or clinic will be happy to tell you about the qualifications and specialties of their counselors and therapists without charge, and probably over the phone. Do some research before you jump in. Check on their accreditation and licensing with the State Board, especially if it is not a religiously sponsored service.

The religiously sponsored services are not in the business of forcing any particular religious viewpoint on you. If any counselor does so, or attempts to force some anti-religious point of view on you, go to someone else.

If you suggest counseling for your intended, I would start with the name of one of the religiously sponsored services or get a recommendation from your pastor, priest, or rabbi. If they would really rather not go to a religiously related counselor, find some other accredited service. Hotlines for various disorders can also give you names and sources of help.

Glossary

Abuse: To use wrongly or improperly; misuse. To hurt or injure by maltreatment; ill-use. To assail with contemptuous, coarse, or insulting words; revile. Physical abuse includes hitting, bruising, kicking, choking, slapping, squeezing so hard as to cause pain, pulling hair, or any action that causes pain and suffering to you. Mental or psychological abuse means causing you to experience terror, fear for your life or physical safety, or causing you to feel revulsion or horror by making you watch the torture of an animal or the destruction of some favorite thing. It may also include causing you to feel that you are the cause of the abuser's destructive behavior, or are the rightful target of their rage when you are not. Verbal abuse is using words to punish, revile, and demean you. You may begin to feel as if the abuser's descriptions of you are true because of the violence of the language and its repetition. That is the idea. You become what you are told you are. This is especially toxic when children are the targets of parental verbal abuse. Sexual abuse is touching, penetrating, or fondling especially of breast or genital areas when the person cannot say no because of age or physical inability. It includes rape, molestation, or unwanted petting. Again, it is particularly harmful to children when perpetrated by someone they are supposed to be able to trust. The victim often concludes that they must have been at fault for something this bad to happen to them. Therefore this trauma, whether forced on a child or adult, should always be treated with counseling or therapy to undo the damage and promote recovery.

ACOA: (Adult Children Of Alcoholics) Adults who grew up in the family of an alcoholic or alcoholics have a whole range of reactions to that toxic upbringing. They have a far higher chance of becoming alcoholics themselves and/or marrying an addict. If they do not, they have to deal with the shame of that childhood, the secretiveness and hiding of emotions, and the codependency that often results. There are support groups for ACOAs and professional counselors who specialize in these problems.

Anorexia Nervosa: A medical condition in which a person has an abnormal fear of gaining weight or becoming obese. They restrict food intake by eating little or no food and exercising constantly, which leads to excessive weight loss. From five to eighteen percent of victims of this disease die as a result. It primarily affects young women from teenage years on.

Bulimia: A subcategory of Anorexia Nervosa in which people eat large quantities of food in order to hide the fact that they are not eating and then vomit or use laxatives to get rid of the food. Vomiting depletes the body of fluids and potassium, which eventually causes heart damage. Overuse of laxatives can cause abdominal problems as well. These are truly dangerous practices.

Bipolar disorder: Formerly called manic/depressive disorder, it is typified by periods of frantic activity or irritability, followed by listlessness, depression, or melancholy. The wild mood swings and depression are difficult to predict or live with. Treatment with lithium and other drugs often helps, along with counseling. Go to a specialist if you or someone you know has this disorder.

Codependent: A person who becomes part of or related to (dependent on) another person's addictive behavior. The person who has the problem, whether it is alcoholism, workaholism, over-controlling, physical or verbal violence, or sexual or even religious abusiveness, causes the rest of the family to adapt to their behavior in some way in order to survive. The family members become outer-directed and codependent as a result. They may become addicts themselves; they may become pleasers; and they often become controlling in order to feel less out of control. They develop a whole range of compulsive behaviors. I discuss some of this in Chapter 2. One of the best discussions is in Bradshaw's *Bradshaw On: The Family,* listed in the Bibliography.

Positive communication: Communication that conveys accurate content in a way that does not demean either of the people talking. Positive communication is lovingly truthful, builds other people up, is kind, does not manipulate, and is respectful of other people's feelings and ideas. It is full of positive statements like, "I really like her, she seems like she would be fun," or, "Skating looks so beautiful, you would really have to be strong to do it." It is mature and secure. You know if you are around someone who is a positive communicator. You feel good about them and about yourself. You feel encouraged after talking to them, and you feel like they have listened and understood what you said and felt.

Negative communication: Communication that conveys accurate or inaccurate content in a way that demeans one or both of the people talking. Negative communication may tell the truth but in a way that hurts the one it is about; it tears other people down, it is unkind, it manipulates, and it is disrespectful of other people's feelings and ideas. It is full of negative statements like, "I hate her, she's a jerk," or, "Skating sucks, it's for wusses." It is immature and self centered. You know if you around someone who is a negative communicator by the way you feel. You feel worse about yourself. You feel put down, discouraged, and like the person didn't care to listen to you or consider your feelings. You may feel dirty after talking to a negative communicator, like you've been dragged through the mud.

Dysfunctional: Abnormal or impaired functioning of a bodily system or organ. When applied to families, it refers to families in which normal, loving relationships are distorted by mental illness, alcoholism, or abuse. Sometimes harsh or repressive religious beliefs are involved. The result is faulty or "toxic" parenting, in which children learn to hide emotions, deal in deceptions to avoid punishment, and keep secrets. They may need to learn from scratch how to love and be open to emotions. Counseling is usually necessary to help victims overcome this dysfunctional upbringing. See *Bradshaw On: The Family.*

Passive/aggressive behavior: As the name suggests, a person who is passive/aggressive learns at an early edge that direct confrontation with a parent or older sibling is too painful, so they adopt a strategy of being passive or pleasing in response to conflict. But in swallowing their anger, they either internalize it to the point that it actually causes illnesses such as heart disease, etc., or they redirect it in aggressive behavior toward others, or both.

Suggested Reading

This is not an exhaustive list, but rather a listing of some of the most helpful books on the subjects discussed in this book. The subjects are listed alphabetically. Some may be out of print but are available at libraries.

Alcoholism

Alcoholics Anonymous. *The Big Book*. New York, NY. Available through AA (see Appendix B).

Bradshaw, John. *Bradshaw On: The Family*. Deerfield Beach, FL. Health Communications. I'll list this book several times; it is very helpful.

Johnson, Vernon E. *I'll Quit Tomorrow*. San Francisco, CA. Harper and Row. Also available through AA.

Johnson, Vernon. *Intervention: How to Help Someone Who Doesn't Want Help*. Minneapolis, MN. Johnson Institute Books.

Vaughn, Joe. *Family Intervention: Hope for Families Struggling with Alcohol and Drugs*. Louisville. Westminster/John Knox Press. Also has suggestions for dealing with anorexia/bulimia, gambling, and violence.

Adult Children of Alcoholics (or Addicts)

Beattie, Melodie. *Codependent No More*. New York, NY. Harper and Row. A classic, told by someone who has really been there.

Bradshaw, John. *Bradshaw On: The Family*. Deerfield Beach, FL. Health Communications Inc. I'll list this book several times, it is particularly helpful in understanding this syndrome and codependency.

Friel, John; and Linda Friel. *Adult Children—The Secrets of Dysfunctional Families*. Deerfield Beach, FL. Health Communications Inc.

Friends In Recovery. *The 12 Steps For Adult Children*. San Diego, CA. Recovery Publications. Available through AA or CoRe (see Appendix B).

Woititz, Janet G. *Adult Children of Alcoholics*. Deerfield Beach,
    FL. Health Communications Inc.
Norwood, Robin. *Women Who Love Too Much: When You Keep
    Hoping He'll Change*. Los Angeles, CA. J. P. Tarcher.
    Distributed by St. Martins Press, New York.

Communication In Marriage
Ball, Robert R. *The "I Feel" Formula*. Waco, TX. Word, Inc.
Dobson, James. *Love Must Be Tough*. Waco, TX. Word, Inc.
Dobson, James. *Emotions: Can You Trust Them?* Ventura, CA.
    Regal Books.
Gray, John T. *Men Are From Mars, Women Are From Venus*. New
    York, NY. Harper Collins.
Harris, Thomas A. *I'm OK—You're OK*. New York, NY. Harper and
    Row.
Shedd, Charlie. *Talk To Me!* Garden City, NY. Doubleday.

Divorce
Gray, John T. *Mars and Venus Starting Over*. New York, NY.
    Harper Collins.
Laney, Carl; William Heth; Thomas Edgar; and Larry Richards.
    Divorce and Remarriage: Four Christian Views. Downers
    Grove, IL. InterVarsity Press.
Sandvig, Karen J. *Adult Children of Divorce*. Dallas, TX. Word
    Publishing.
Smoke, Jim. *Growing Through Divorce*. Eugene, OR. Harvest
    House.
Smoke, Jim. *Suddenly Single*. Old Tappan, NJ. Fleming H. Revell.
Whiteman, Thomas; and Debbie Barr. *When Your Son Or Daughter
    Is Going Through A Divorce*. Nashville, TN. Thomas Nelson
    publishers.

Dysfunctional Families
Bradshaw, John. *Bradshaw On: The Family*. Deerfield Beach, FL.
    Health Communications Inc.

Bradshaw, John. *Healing The Shame Within*. Deerfield Beach, FL. Health Communications Inc.

Townsend, John; and Henry Cloud. *Boundaries: When To Say Yes And When To Say No*. Grand Rapids, MI. Zondervan.

Norwood, Robin. *Women Who Love Too Much: When You Keep Hoping He'll Change*. Los Angeles, CA. J. P. Tarcher. Distributed by St. Martins Press, New York.

Marriage, General

Lieberman, Carole; and Lisa Cool. *Bad Boys: Why We Love Them, How To Live With Them, and When To Leave Them*. Viking Press, Penguin Books.

Schlessinger, Laura. *Ten Stupid Things Women Do To Mess Up Their Lives*. New York, NY. Villard Books.

Schlessinger, Laura. *Ten Stupid Things Men Do To Mess Up Their Lives*. New York, NY. Cliff Street Books.

Shedd, Charlie. *Letters To Karen*. Nashville, TN. Abingdon Press.

Shedd, Charlie, *Letters To Philip*. Old Tappan, NJ. Fleming H. Revell, Spire Books.

Money

Shedd, Charlie. *Letters To Karen*. Nashville, TN. Abingdon Press.

Shedd, Charlie, *Letters To Philip*. Old Tappan, NJ. Fleming H. Revell, Spire
    Books

Sex

Cook, Philip W. *Abused Men: The Hidden Side of Violence*. Praeger.

Engel, Beverly. *The Right To Innocence: Healing the Trauma of Childhood Sexual Abuse*. New York, NY. St. Martins Press. On sex abuse of women.

Hunter, Mic. *Abused Boys*. Lexington, MA. Lexington Books.

Penner, Clifford; and Joyce Penner. *The Gift Of Sex*. Waco, TX. Word, Inc.

Wheat, Ed. *Sexual Happiness in Marriage*.

Raising Children

Cline, Foster; and Jim Fay. *Parenting with Love and Logic.*
    Colorado Springs, CO. NavPress.
Cline, Foster; and Jim Fay. *Parenting Teens with Love and Logic.*
    Colorado Springs, CO. NavPress.
Dobson, James. *Dare To Discipline*. Waco, TX. Word, Inc.

For Further Information

John Lacy is available for
speaking engagements and workshops.

Send Inquires to:
**email: john.lacy@gte.net
or spiritp@teleport.com
Fax:
503-235-8135
Voice
503-625-4420**

To order additional copies of

Discover Love

Book: $13.95   Shipping/Handling: $3.50

Contact: SPIRIT PRESS
3324 N.E. Peerless Place
Portland, Oregon 97232
Phone: 800-507-BOOK (2665)
Fax: 503-235-8135
E-mail: spiritp@teleport.com